# Archaeology

## Digging Deeper to Learn About the Past

## A Middle School Unit of Study

by
Judith Cochran

Incentive Publications, Inc.
Nashville, Tennessee

*Illustrated by Gayle S. Harvey*
*Cover by Geoffrey Brittingham*

Library of Congress Catalog Card Number: 99-71591
ISBN 0-86530-436-X

PRINTED IN THE UNITED STATES OF AMERICA

# Table of Contents

# PREFACE

*Archaeology* is a middle school unit of study that brings history alive by revealing parallels between everyday life in ancient times and everyday life today. From the beginning of the unit, students are asked to investigate and interpret artifacts from their own lives and homes. Common threads of personal experience are linked with each aspect of the archaeological process. The meticulous record-keeping techniques introduced and the various ways of interpreting data integrate a variety of sciences and analytical thinking into the process.

Critical thinking is a natural part of archaeology since every part of an excavation must be interpreted. As such, critical thinking is an integral part of this unit. Science experiments, mathematics, written reports, panel discussions, and the creation of and participation in an actual dig are all included. With all of these meaningful experiences, the culmination of the unit is an archaeological conference at which the results of each excavation are reported. A museum display exhibits the artifacts and projects completed throughout the unit.

*Archaeology* is unique in its scope. Middle school students will benefit from the hands-on activities that bring complex concepts to life. As a naturally integrated unit, archaeology consolidates separate subject areas into a conceptual whole that is easily taught by teachers of different subjects, or those involved in a core curriculum. A pretest and/or post-test provides a further measure of student growth.

The depth of understanding achieved across the curriculum is what middle school educators have long envisioned. With *Archaeology*, it becomes reality.

# The Study of Ancient Life

---

***Vocabulary:***

**artifact**—an object created or produced by humans and then left behind
**ballistics**—the study of projectiles; a projectile launched by hand or machine
**catalogue**—to clean, number, organize, and store artifacts for study
**destruction layer**—layer of ruin caused by enemy attack, fire, or natural disaster such as an earthquake or volcanic activity
**excavate**—to remove or expose artifacts by digging in a systematic manner
**locus**—locality of place; a specific location in which artifacts are found
**locus sheet**—card attached to artifacts detailing when and where they were found
**midden**—ancient garbage pit
**seal**—small inscribed stone used to imprint official documents
**site**—a place or area to be excavated

---

## Chapter 1

### Discovering Aspects of Ancient Life through Artifacts

The word *archaeology* comes from the Greek language and means "to study what is ancient." Archaeologists excavate *artifacts*—including bones, pottery, coins, building materials, and other ancient remains—to learn as much as possible about the lives of people from the past.

All aspects of ancient life are of interest to archaeologists, including:

- *how people lived*—the tools they used, the work they did, the pottery they created, their belief systems, their language, their medicine, the food they ate, the games they played, how they spent their leisure time, how they communicated, and how they and traveled.

- *where people lived and how it affected their lives*—their homes, their style of architecture, the building materials they used, the clothes they wore, and the purpose of their buildings.

Interestingly, gold, precious metals, and jewels are not as important to archaeologists, because they fail to reveal much about the daily lives of the people who owned them. By interpreting the everyday artifacts people have left behind, archaeologists can learn a great deal about the day-to-day lives of our ancestors. Although artifacts answer some questions, they often raise many more. That is why the archaeological process is an ongoing one. One interpretation of the artifacts may hold true only until new artifacts are unearthed. In many ways, the study of archaeology is like unraveling a mystery or piecing together an ancient jigsaw puzzle with many of the pieces missing. And that is what makes it so interesting and rewarding!

8

## Locus

When and where artifacts are found is very important to archaeologists. The place where artifacts are found, or the *locus*, is identified on a *locus sheet* that is attached to the artifacts or the container in which they are stored. This locus sheet stays with the artifacts as they are *catalogued*.

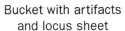

Bucket with artifacts
and locus sheet

The artifacts are cleaned and numbered. Every artifact is given a different number, and these numbers are written on the locus sheet.

Every locus sheet has a complex number on it. This number reflects the details about when and where the artifacts were found.

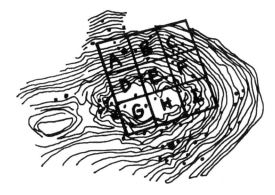

Map of a site with fields noted: The fields are divided into squares, and each square is given a letter.

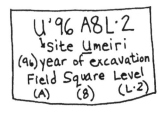

Within a square, each layer is also given a number.

When the archaeologists begin studying the artifacts, where the artifacts are found becomes especially important because the location may reveal the story of the *site*. For example, when *excavating* a site in Jordan, a *seal* the size of a pebble was found. This seal was the key to understanding the site. As it turned out, the seal (which was almost mistaken for a rock and tossed aside) bore the name of an important ruler. This seal revealed that the site was the main administration center of the region.

All of this information was available because:
1. There were walls to large buildings with no household artifacts (so archaeologists knew they weren't homes).
2. Seals and other artifacts from the same time period pointed to a place where business was conducted.
3. The seal of the high ranking official conclusively identified the site as an administrative center.

None of this would have been possible were it not for the locus of the artifacts.

*Archaeology*
Copyright ©1999 by Incentive Publications, Inc., Nashville, TN.

## Artifacts—Lost or Thrown Away

Usually, the artifacts archaeologists find were either lost or thrown away. In the case of a site in Jordan, the artifacts recovered were lost or dropped when the complex was attacked and destroyed by fire. A thick layer of charred wood, bricks, and rubble told of the fire. Hundreds of *ballistics*, projectiles, and metal tips of lances, spears, and arrows (one found with the charred bones of a man) proved that the complex was attacked.

At other sites, some of the most productive areas are garbage pits, or *middens*. There is abundant evidence in them to understand many aspects of the everyday life of an ancient culture—the food eaten, dishes and utensils used, and pastimes (i.e., pipe stems mean they smoked, dice mean they played games of chance, and so forth).

By closely analyzing each artifact and where it came from, the story of life in the past comes to light.

The artifacts that archaeologists find are usually items that were lost or thrown away.

# Activity: Locus Sheet

## Materials
- Student Page 111 (copy on card stock or heavy paper for best results)
- large and small resealable plastic bags
- marking pens
- butcher paper (for teacher and students)
- scissors

## Discussion

(As the discussion proceeds, the teacher should record students' ideas on a large piece of butcher paper.) Discuss different aspects of the students' lives that archaeologists might study 1,000 years from now—tools used, jobs, food, clothing, homes, use of leisure time, games played, and so forth. Then discuss what kinds of present-day artifacts archaeologists might find to tell about each aspect of their lives. Remind students that most of the artifacts unearthed will be those that were lost or thrown away. List the aspects and corresponding artifacts on the butcher paper. Keep the butcher paper for a follow-up activity.

10

*NOTE: Encourage critical thinking. Artifacts we take for granted may be difficult for future archaeologists to interpret. For example, how will a pizza box be interpreted if archaeologists can't read the writing? If no pizza remains are present, how will they know its function?*

**Student Page 111**

Each student receives two resealable plastic bags—one large, one small. Discuss the sites in their homes where lost and discarded artifacts might be found.

Lost artifacts might be found between sofa or chair cushions, under beds, in junk drawers, or on closet floors.

Discarded artifacts might be found in wastebaskets, trash cans, or where items are stored for garage sales, flea markets, or to be given to charities. Attics may also have discarded artifacts.

Students will use one bag to collect artifacts from a "lost" site and the other to collect discarded items from a "trash" site.

*NOTE: It is important for students to gather all artifacts from a single locus for each bag— for example, from the family room sofa and the bathroom wastebasket instead of all sofas or wastebaskets in the house—otherwise the results will not be reliable.*

Students cut and fill out site information on locus sheets and place one in each bag. Once they are home and the locus has been determined, students should record that information before excavating. When all artifacts have been excavated, students then draw and label each artifact. They should then bring their artifact bags back to school.

# Follow-Up Activity

## Materials
- students with artifact bags and corresponding locus sheets
- 24" x 24" pieces of butcher paper (one per group of four to five students)
- marking pens (various colors)
- teacher's butcher paper information from previous activity (see page 10)
- shoeboxes to hold each group's artifact bags for future use

## Discussion

(Teacher writes on butcher paper from previous activity in a different color pen.) List some artifacts students were able to find from each category. Write them in a different color next to the brainstormed artifacts from the previous activity.

Discuss how students' artifacts compared to those brainstormed. How were they different? How were they similar? What conclusions can be drawn about everyday life from the artifacts found? Why were or weren't the brainstormed artifacts found? What limitations do lost and discarded artifacts present?

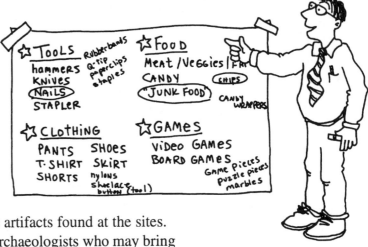

Remind students that this is exactly the kind of work archaeologists do. Their information depends only on the artifacts found at the sites. They keep detailed records for future archaeologists who may bring new information and greater insight to the interpretation of a site.

## Student Activity

Students bring their artifact bags with completed locus sheets together in groups of four or five. On the 24" x 24" pieces of butcher paper, they will categorize and tally their combined artifacts, recording where and what they found. Care must be taken to keep the artifacts and locus sheets in their original bags. As a group, students should draw conclusions about the types of artifacts found in each location and what they think the artifacts mean. Students then share their results with the rest of the class.

*NOTE: Each group stores their artifact bags in a labeled shoebox for future analysis. (See Who's Who on Activity Page 16 and Student Page 112)*

## Extension

Make a graph of the artifacts most and least frequently found. Brainstorm for reasons why some artifacts are more plentiful than others.

# The Study of Ancient Life

---

## *Vocabulary:*

**ceramic technologist**—one who studies all aspects of how and where ancient pottery was made

**dendrochronologist**—one who studies tree rings

**desiccate**—to dry out completely; dehydrate

**find**—any archaeological discovery (used as a noun, a find)

**flotation**—means by which ancient pollen grains are found

**forensic archaeologist**—one who studies human body remains to determine such things as diet, health, age, and disease

**glyphs**—stylized picture writing (for example, the Egyptian hieroglyphs)

**Neanderthal**—an extinct Stone Age species of human

**numismatist**—one who studies coins

**ostraca**—broken piece of pottery on which there is writing

**paleobotanist**—one who studies ancient plant remains and fossils

**paleographer**—one who studies ancient inscriptions and documents

**potsherd or sherd**—broken piece of pottery

**Pueblo Indians**—a group of Native Americans who built multi-tiered adobe or stone housing complexes in the Southwestern United States

**stele**—stone marker or pillar inscribed with writing or pictures

---

## Chapter 2

### Who's Who

Because archaeologists study all aspects of life, there are many specialists in the field. Archaeology is a uniquely cooperative science, dependent upon the detailed analysis of artifacts from many scientific disciplines. Each specialist adds a piece to the puzzle.

**Forensic Archaeologist**

A *forensic archaeologist* is one who studies human body remains to determine such things as diet, health, age, and disease. These scientists have examined mummified remains from ancient Egypt and have discovered that people suffered from lung ailments caused by breathing the smoke from their cooking fires and inhaling the fine particles of desert sand.

Forensic archaeologists can determine from bones whether or not a person did a great deal of physical labor by noting where the key ligaments were attached to the bones, and how large they appeared. From weakness and wear on vertebrae, they can tell if a person was sick as a child or had done work too hard and heavy for their body. The pitting of the skull can indicate

13

malnutrition, and worn teeth and jaw bone deterioration can reveal an older person with gum disease. Undeveloped bones in the fingers and skull signal to scientists that they are looking at the remains of a child or adolescent.

Some ancient medical practices continue to astound archaeologists and doctors alike. Some skulls show evidence of ancient surgery! Holes were drilled into the skulls of living people. Judging from the healed bone around these holes, many patients survived the procedure. Why the practice was used remains a mystery.

Skull with bored holes. The healed bone shows that the patient survived the procedure.

Vertebrae with a spear point embedded in it reveals the likely cause of death.

On rare occasions, bodies thousands of years old are found preserved in ice or bogs or by *desiccation*. These glimpses into the lives of ancient people provide forensic archaeologists with a wealth of information. They learn about diet by analyzing stomach remains. Worms and other intestinal parasites are sometimes found. Even wear on the fingernails is considered and shows whether or not the person was a laborer.

## Paleobotanist

A *paleobotanist* is one who studies ancient plant remains and fossils. Fossilized pollen is often collected through a process called *flotation*, during which ancient plant remains are left floating when dirt from ancient sites is mixed with water. The pollen is collected by a fine wire mesh.

Ancient microscopic pollen grains reveal the kinds of plants in the area.

A significant *find* was discovered when paleobotanists analyzed the dirt from a *Neanderthal* burial site and found that it contained pollen from flowers! This meant that flowers were included in the burial, much like in burials today. Until this discovery, the Neanderthals were thought to be more animal-like than human. The placing of flowers in the grave was an act of sentiment once thought impossible. This revelation caused archaeologists to rethink their conclusions about the Neanderthals.

## Paleographer

A *paleographer* is one who studies ancient inscriptions and documents by interpreting ancient languages and *glyphs*. Many important inscriptions were carved on *stele* as well as tomb and cave walls. Smaller, more personal records were written on *ostraca* when papyrus or other paper-like surfaces were unavailable.

Paleographers can also decipher inscriptions on seals. Seals of officials were attached to important documents. The extent of political influence in an area can be understood by interpreting the language or style of the inscription on the seal.

Some Mayan glyphs have been difficult to decipher.

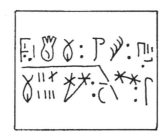

This Minoan Linear A script has yet to be deciphered.

This cuneiform medical text lists cures for illnesses.

## Numismatist

A *numismatist* is one who studies coins (and often medals). When coins are found at a site, they immediately date that site as no earlier than the most recent coin. Coins were minted differently in antiquity than they are now. Each emperor or ruler minted coins with his likeness on them. Whether or not they bear a date, by recognizing the likeness on the coin, the numismatist is likely to know the dates and length of reign for the ruler depicted.

Coins help date archaeological sites because numismatists know the dates of the rulers (or other distinguishing marks) pictured on them.

## Ceramic Technologist

A *ceramic technologist* is one who studies *potsherds* to understand the manufacturing techniques of ancient pottery. By far, the majority of artifacts found at sites are potsherds. This is because clay that has been heated is quite durable and not subject to decay.

This specialist "reads" the pottery and can tell at a glance the type of container the sherds came from, the historic period to which it belongs, and the people who made it.

## Dendrochronologist

A *dendrochronologist* is a person who studies tree rings. This study is very useful in dating wood remains. Depending on yearly weather conditions, annual tree rings vary in width each growing season. Scientists can look at these rings and determine the age of the object. This method was used exten-

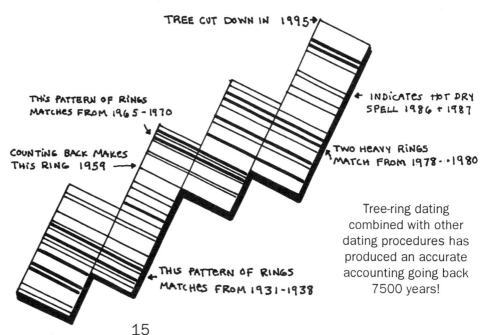

TREE CUT DOWN IN 1995

THIS PATTERN OF RINGS MATCHES FROM 1965-1970

COUNTING BACK MAKES THIS RING 1959

INDICATES HOT DRY SPELL 1986 + 1987

TWO HEAVY RINGS MATCH FROM 1978-1980

THIS PATTERN OF RINGS MATCHES FROM 1931-1938

Tree-ring dating combined with other dating procedures has produced an accurate accounting going back 7500 years!

15

sively in dating *Pueblo Indian* sites in the American Southwest because of the wooden beams and ladders used throughout their building complexes. Tree-ring analysis proved invaluable in accurately dating these Pueblo remains, since other dating methods often provide only general reference to dates. (See Chapter 15, *Context, Scientific Procedures, and Evolution of Objects*.)

## Activity: Who's Who and Specialist Report

### Materials
- Student Page 112
- Student Page 113
- artifacts from Chapter 1, Activity Page 11

### Discussion
(Teacher writes responses on board.) Discuss the artifacts with which each specialist would work. What questions would they ask about each type of artifact? What conclusions could they draw about ancient life from studying their special artifacts?

Brainstorm about present-day artifacts that each specialist would study in the future. What conclusions could they draw about life today by studying them?

### Student Page 112
In pairs, students analyze their individual artifacts. They draw and label them under the appropriate specialty, then devise questions each specialist would ask about them.

Next, students divide into groups of six pairs (twelve students). The group reviews the information on Student Page 112, adding insight and questions to those each pair of students wrote. They then brainstorm ideas about what conclusions can be drawn from the artifacts in each area of specialty.

### Student Page 113
Each pair of students in the group becomes a team of specialists and analyzes all the group's artifacts in their specialty. They present their conclusions to the group, then write a report on their findings.

## Extension

Students are divided into six groups. Each group is assigned a specialty area. They either analyze all artifacts already in bags or gather other artifacts (and complete a Locus Sheet for each site; see Student Page 111). Once they have reached conclusions about their artifacts, they present a report to the class.

# How Do We Know about the Past?

---

### *Vocabulary:*

**antiquity**—ancient times

**cartouche**—oval enclosure of royal name written in hieroglyphics

**codices**—volume or collection of manuscripts

**cuneiform**—first known form of writing recorded on wet clay tablets with a wedge-shaped reed pen

**hieroglyphics**—picture-symbol writing developed in ancient Egypt

**history**—the advent of writing demarcates history

**oracle bones**—inscribed bones that are heated in order to decipher the cracks and foretell the future

**papyrus**—first form of paper, made from the papyrus plant in ancient Egypt

**parchment**—paper-like surface made from processed animal skins

**petroglyphs**—pictures etched or painted onto rocks and cliffs

**prehistory**—prehistory refers to time before written history

**quipu** (KEY-poo)—knotted strings used for primitive record keeping

**scribe**—person who wrote documents, a high-ranking post in antiquity

**stylus**—sharp metal writing tool used by Romans to write on wax tablets

---

## Chapter 3

### Deciphering Ancient Writing

**Prehistory versus History**

The separation of *history* from *prehistory* is marked by the advent of writing and the ability of people to leave behind written records. In prehistoric times, there was no writing, so only artifacts can tell the story of these ancient societies—mainly tools and ancient campsites where animal, as well as human, bones give insight into everyday life.

The closest thing to writing left by prehistoric people were *petroglyphs* and cave paintings. Both forms of expression reveal a great deal about the animals that existed at the time and provide a quick glimpse into the lives of our ancestors. For example, petroglyphs of various animals in the Sahara desert reveal a climate and terrain very different from the parched desert of today. Long before it had become a vast expanse of barren sand, the Sahara had a temperate climate with enough water to support woodlands, grasslands, lakes, animals, and humans.

Cave paintings in present day France, Spain, and other prehistoric sites depict not only animals, but also show the outlines of human hands with parts of fingers missing. Some archaeologists believe the hand outlines suggest ritual finger amputation. Others believe the outlines were made as a form of identification, with fingers bent to distinguish one person from another.

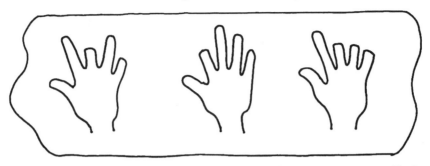

Truncated fingers on hand outlines in prehistoric caves were most likely for identification, though some believe it shows ritual finger amputation.

### Notched Sticks and Quipus

Before writing and numbers were invented, ingenious ways of marking the passage of time were devised using notches carved into sticks, or groups of knotted strings called a *quipu*.

The notched sticks served as a record-keeping device to count animals or other commodities. They also were used as a primitive means of communication. A "talking stick" was notched as the sender told a courier what to say. Once at his destination, the courier would "read" the notches on the stick, which reminded him of each part of the message. Notched sticks were used by people throughout the world before the written word was invented.

Quipus were used as primitive calendars and also as a way of recording events, keeping accounts, or sending messages. There is a story about an ancient military leader who left his troops, but was going to rejoin them. To assure them he would return, he left behind a long leather quipu with 60 knots and instructions to untie one knot each day. When all knots were untied, that was the day he would return.

Some quipus were made of colored cords of varying lengths; each length and color had a special meaning. In ancient times, the Inca of Peru made frequent use of quipus, and, in fact, they still use them today.

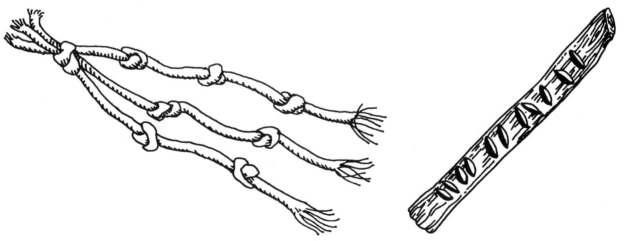

Quipus and notched sticks were used as primitive calendars and record-keeping devices.

18

*Archaeology*
Copyright ©1999 by Incentive Publications, Inc., Nashville, TN.

**Development of Writing**

Writing was invented as trade between cities and states developed. People needed to record the details of their exchanges—what items were sent, to whom, how many, for how much, and so forth.

With the advent of writing came the need for specialists to legibly write everything down. Thus, the job of the *scribe* was born. Scribes throughout antiquity recorded all kinds of information—official government edicts, trade agreements, legal decisions, religious rites, prayers, and general letters. They were an elite educated class employed by government officials and anyone else in need of written records.

Scribes in Egypt carried a scribal palette, consisting of a box with reed pens, cakes of red and black ink, and a place to store extra rolls of *papyrus*.

Scribes in ancient Egypt sat cross-legged and spread papyrus across their legs to write.

The scribe's palette included two cakes of ink—one red and one black—reed pens, a knife to sharpen them, and a roll of extra papyrus.

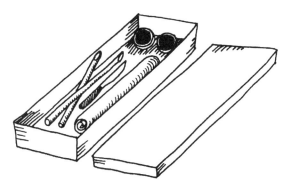

To identify a communiqué as coming from a specific official, a seal inscribed with the name of the official was fixed to the document. Two types of seals were most common—the cylinder seal and the stamp seal. Cylinder seals were rolled onto a wet clay surface to leave an imprint. They often had a hole in their middle so they could be worn around the neck. Stamp seals were simply pressed onto a surface. Some were worn as finger rings.

Stamp seal         Cylinder seal         Impression left from cylinder seal rolled on wet clay.

**Cuneiform, Hieroglyphics, and the Rosetta Stone**

*Cuneiform*, the first known form of writing, was developed in ancient Sumer (present-day Iraq). The word cuneiform literally means "wedge shaped" and describes the wedge-shaped reed pen used to mark the wet clay tablets. Fortunately, many of these clay tablets have survived the ravages of time and provide archaeologists with detailed information about trade and other matters pertaining to the people of the Mediterranean area. Many Near Eastern civilizations adapted the Sumerian cuneiform script to write their respective languages.

19

The ancient Egyptians developed their own writing called *hieroglyphics,* which they recorded on stone monuments and *stele.* These stone markers were used to inscribe important information meant to last long periods of time. Stele tell of important edicts or famous battles; they also record laws and accomplishments.

For centuries, no one could decipher hieroglyphics because there was no way to compare it to other writing that was already understood. It wasn't until Napoleon's army discovered a large stone stele with both ancient Greek (which was understood) and hieroglyphics on it that experts could decipher the ancient Egyptian writing. Because the stele was found near the Egyptian town of Rosetta, it became known as the Rosetta Stone.

Cuneiform is made by pressing a wedge-shaped pen into wet clay.

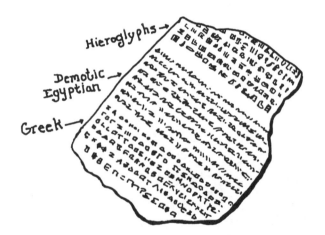

The Rosetta Stone helped scholars decipher hieroglyphics by comparing them to the known Greek text on the stone.

When a person's name appeared in hieroglyphics, it was surrounded by an oval shape known as a *cartouche.* This oval got its name from Napoleon's soldiers, who likened the shape to that of a powder charge used in their cannons which was called a cartouche.

This cartouche contains the name "Ptolmys," which was the family to which Cleopatra belonged.

20

**Writing Surfaces**

Hieroglyphics were also written on *papyrus*, which is a stiff paper made from the papyrus plant. Thin strips of the papyrus stem were laid in a cross-hatched manner, then pressed with a heavy weight to extract all water and allow the natural glue in the plant to release and hold the paper together. Once dry, papyrus was written upon and rolled into scrolls for easy storage. Our word paper comes from the word papyrus.

Papyrus was used throughout the Mediterranean. It was expensive to import and was very stiff and brittle (imagine trying to fold a straw place mat), but it was popular because it was so convenient to use and easy to store. To remedy the pitfalls of papyrus, *parchment* was developed to serve as paper. Parchment was made from thin layers of processed animal skins. A great deal of work went into making it, but it could be made anywhere sheep, goats, or other such animals were raised. Papyrus, however, was available only where the papyrus plant grew, primarily in Egypt.

Because paper was so expensive, only completed documents were written on it. Notes or other informal writings were committed to pieces of broken pottery called *ostraca*. Many writings of the common people were written on ostraca.

To solve the problem of expensive paper, the Romans developed a portable and reusable writing apparatus. A wooden tablet coated with bee's wax was etched with a pointed *stylus*, and erased by smoothing the wax. Thus people were able to use a writing surface countless times without wasting valuable paper.

The Roman wax tablet and stylus was one of the first portable and reusable writing surfaces.

The main problem with documents written on papyrus or parchment was that they were likely to deteriorate or be destroyed over time. This happened both as a result of natural aging processes and also because of disastrous events. Famous libraries in the ancient world—Alexandria, Ephesus, and Constantinople—once housed countless volumes of papyrus and parchment scrolls and *codices*. When these libraries were destroyed (usually by fire), unique manuscripts were lost forever. However, many clay tablets, on which cuneiform was written, and stone stele have been preserved, even though they may have been cracked or broken over time.

21

Periodically, archaeologists stumble upon caches of papyrus or parchment documents that shed light on books and other writings once thought lost. Others provide insight to earlier documents from which only later translations have survived. For example, many books in the Bible had been translated into Greek long after they were originally written. In some cases the earliest known manuscripts of the Bible were the Greek translations. That is why discovery of the Dead Sea Scrolls was so significant. For the first time, there were earlier manuscripts of the Old Testament to compare to the later Greek texts.

The "Temple Scroll" and the jar in which it was found
was one of the first of the Dead Sea Scrolls to be discovered.

**The Development of Chinese Writing**

Virtually all writing developed as picture-symbols (for example, the letters in our alphabet), which stood for sounds. This made for a manageable alphabet with a limited number of letters from which all words could be made. The exception is the development of Chinese characters, which convey ideas and things instead of sounds. This makes for a complex system of writing using hundreds of different characters, each representing a different concept. This system was used and standardized for hundreds of years. Though the characters used today are still rooted in this ancient concept, some characters now represent sounds as well.

The earliest Chinese writing appeared on *oracle bones*, on which questions to the gods were written. These bones were then heated over a flame, and the pattern of cracks on the bone and through the writing were interpreted to answer the questions.

Chinese oracle bones were heated, and the resulting cracks were analyzed to foretell the future.

The Chinese also wrote on silk cloth because it was easily compacted and stored, but it was also very expensive. Later, they wrote books on bamboo strips fastened together with cord. Chinese characters had to be written in columns from top to bottom on the bamboo strips.

(Today, Chinese is still written in columns.) These books soon became awkward because of their size and weight. So, independent of the Egyptians, the Chinese began experimenting with a writing surface that was less cumbersome. In the end, they discovered how to make paper from rag pulp (which is similar to the process of making paper today!).

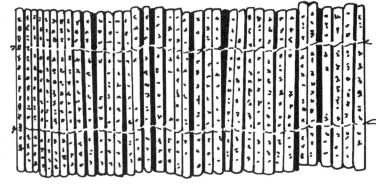

Bamboo books proved cumbersome, but writing in columns remains the Chinese way today.

## Difficult to Decipher Writings

There still exists ancient writing that experts have trouble deciphering. It wasn't until 1952 that the Mycenaean script known as "Linear B" was deciphered by a British architect named Michael Ventris. He noted that it was used to write an early form of Greek. The "Linear A" script, however, has yet to be understood.

Another script yet to be deciphered is from the Indus Valley area in present-day India and Pakistan. Comprised of *glyphs*, which seem to be a form of picture writing, the symbols appear to have several different disconnected meanings, and this presents the major obstacle to unlocking the code. The writing also appears primarily on seals which are limited to only a few symbols each. So far, scholars have only named the language and know that it is read from right to left.

Indus Valley glyphs are most often found on seals with short inscriptions, making it difficult to find clues to decipher it.

23

# Activity: Deciphering Ancient Writing

## Materials
- Student Page 114

## Discussion
Discuss similarities and differences among cuneiform, hieroglyphics, and the evolution of the other alphabets on Student Page 114.

## Student Page 114
Each student studies hieroglyphics and writes his or her own name in the cartouche. After they have studied the different alphabets, encourage them to use one to complete a class assignment or to compare one of the alphabets to our own.

# Activity: Original Rosetta Stone

## Materials
- Student Page 115

## Discussion
Discuss how the discovery of the Rosetta Stone allowed experts to decipher hieroglyphics for the first time. Because the text was written in three scripts—one of which was already known—it made the task possible.

## Student Page 115
Students create their own language or code by entering three scripts of their own.

*(NOTE: It is suggested that they print the message as the first script, write in cursive as the second script, then enter their code as the third script.) Once complete, the students exchange papers and decipher each other's scripts, then detail how they created their codes in a brief report (oral or written).*

# Extensions

## Ancient Number Systems

Encourage students to use Egyptian, Roman or Arabic numerals for some of their math assignments. Discuss the difficulties of using each system instead of our own.

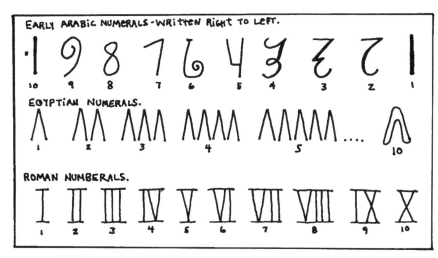

## Clay and Cuneiform

### Materials:

- air-drying clay (available at most hobby stores)
- wooden chop stick or stick carved to leave wedge-shaped marks

Take small slab of clay large enough to fit in the palm and make cuneiform-like markings on it to write a paragraph about the experience. Once finished, lay the slabs out to dry (this will take about a day on each side to ensure complete drying). Then brainstorm about the difficulties involved in storing the clay tablets. (No wonder other, less cumbersome writing surfaces were developed!)

*NOTE: Students can fashion seals from clay as well. They might also construct a stele with the class rules on it.*

Cuneiform writing is made by using a wedge-shaped pen to mark in soft clay.

25

## Quipu

### Materials:

• string of different lengths and colors

In small groups, students experiment with expressing various number concepts, calendars, or recording an event by tying knots on the strings. Once complete, each group reports on their results.

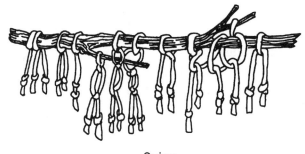

Quipu

## Writing Right to Left

Research the various languages read from right to left, such as Hebrew and Arabic. Discuss how books would be read from back to front. Then have students write English from right to left and give it to others to read.

TFEL OT THGIR HSILGNE GNITIRW YRT

## Egyptian Scribe's Palette

### Materials:

• box (wooden cigar box or small shoe box)
• red and black paint cakes (from watercolor set)
• reed pens
• modern binder, paper, pens, and so forth

Have several small group of students make a replica of an Egyptian scribe's palette, complete with ink cakes, reed pens, and extra papyrus rolls. Then as them to construct the modern-day equivalent of what a scribe carried—for example, a backpack or binder containing paper, pens, and so forth. Students should then note similarities and differences between the two.

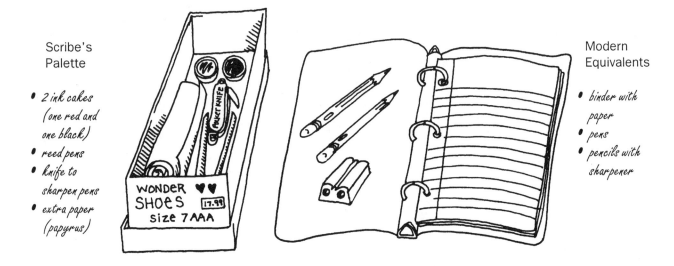

Scribe's Palette

• 2 ink cakes (one red and one black)
• reed pens
• knife to sharpen pens
• extra paper (papyrus)

Modern Equivalents

• binder with paper
• pens
• pencils with sharpener

26

## Roman Wax Tablet and Stylus

### Materials:
- two pieces of wood or cardboard, about 10" x 12" each
- beeswax or wax paper
- sharp dental tool or other instrument to use as a stylus

Construct a tablet with beeswax or waxed paper coating each side. Make a place to carry the stylus in the tablet. Use it to take notes or write about its construction. Make note of its good and bad qualities.

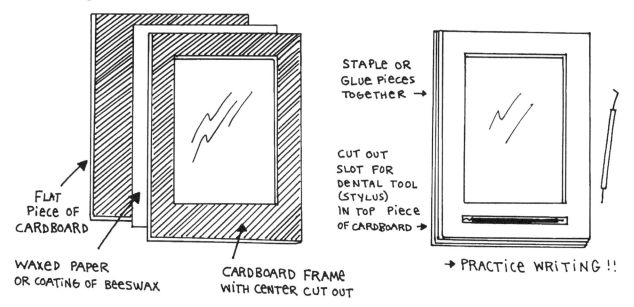

FLAT PieCe OF CARDBOARD

WAXED PAPER OR COATING OF BEESWAX

CARDBOARD FRAME WITH CENTER CUT OUT

STAPLE OR GLUE PieCeS TOGETHER →

CUT OUT SLOT FOR DENTAL TOOL (STYLUS) IN TOP PieCe OF CARDBOARD →

→ PRACTICE WRITING!!

## Chinese Bamboo Book

### Materials:
- popsicle sticks, tongue depressors, or strips of bamboo
- string or light cord
- pen

Construct a bamboo book by lacing together strips of wood or bamboo with a cord or string. Write the steps taken to construct the book on the strips. Make sure to write in columns from top to bottom as the Chinese do.

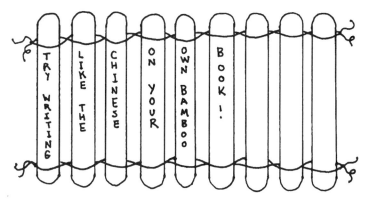

Weave string in and out around the slats. Tie the ends.

27

# How Do We Know about the Past?

---

***Vocabulary:***

**B.C.E.**—stands for "Before the Common Era" and replaces "B.C."

**C.E.**—stands for "Common Era" and replaces "A.D."

**Heinrich Schliemann**—early archaeologist who found Troy using information from *The Iliad*

**Herodotus**—Greek historian who wrote about the ancient civilizations of the Mediterranean region

**Homer and The Iliad**—Greek poet and his poem about the Trojan War

**Julius Caesar**—Roman general and first emperor of Rome

**pharaoh**—ruler of ancient Egypt

**Plato**—Greek philosopher who wrote many books, including those about his teacher Socrates and the island of Atlantis

**platonic**—purely intellectual or spiritual relationship; also refers to the philosophy of Plato

**Pliny**—Roman historian who wrote accurately about the volcanic eruption that buried Pompeii

**Ramses II**—Egyptian pharaoh who lived around 1300 B.C.

**Seven Wonders of the Ancient World**—architectural marvels found in the Mediterranean region and noted by the historian Herodotus

**Socrates**—Greek philosopher who taught by posing questions

**utopia**—place where everything is perfect

---

## Chapter 4

## Historian Accounts

### Reliability of Ancient Records

Historians writing about their own time can give archaeologists great insights into the major events and civilizations of the past. They often write about the little known facts and small details of everyday life that would never be known otherwise. Written records, however, will never provide a true picture of what actually happened. Even when trying to be objective, a historian views the world from a single cultural outlook. Through the ages, it is the victors who usually write the history and, therefore, only their side of the story is told.

For example, *Pharaoh Ramses II* of Egypt in 1300 B.C. had an inscription written on the wall of a temple next to a picture of himself holding a prisoner by the hair. It read:

*I found 2,500 enemy chariots where I had been lying. They were broken to pieces by my horses.*

This quote describes how Ramses II was cut off from his army (a military blunder he had caused himself), and how he had single-handedly destroyed incredible numbers of the enemy to rejoin his troops. Interestingly, the Hittites (who were the Pharaoh's enemy during this battle) record this same battle as a draw. Whom are we to believe?

The text accompanying this picture of Pharaoh Ramses II about to kill his enemies is not a reliable historical account.

Some historians are more reliable than others. The brilliantly successful Roman general and emperor *Julius Caesar* wrote at length about his military campaigns. In them, he detailed his military strategies. They were required reading by students in ancient Rome. Other emperors and generals used them to plan new military campaigns. Julius Caesar's accounts remain a text-book example of military maneuvers and strategy even today. The reliability of ancient writings depends on many factors: the writer, what was written, and why it was written.

## Homer and Heinrich Schliemann

Some ancient writings have been used successfully to locate long-lost sites. About 700 B.C. there lived a Greek poet named *Homer*. He committed to paper the oral story of the Trojan War and called his long poem *The Iliad*. It detailed the gods and heroes who fought a war over Helen, a Greek, being taken to the city of Troy.

Although the legend was over 2,000 years old, an archaeologist named *Heinrich Schliemann* used it to locate the ancient city of Troy in present-day Turkey. Although Schliemann's methods were crude by today's standards, he found many fascinating artifacts. The most famous are a cache of hundreds of gold beads and a gold mask. Though it was later found that his gold ornaments did not date to the time of the Trojan war, the fact remains that Schliemann found the site using *The Iliad* as a guide.

Heinrich Schliemann found this hammered gold mask at Mycenae, and a cache of gold artifacts at the site of ancient Troy. He used Homer's poem *The Iliad* to locate the sites.

29

## Herodotus

*Herodotus* was a Greek historian who lived about 400 B.C. and wrote about many of the Mediterranean civilizations then ruled by the Greeks. He described the *Seven Wonders of the Ancient World*: (1) the pyramids of Egypt, (2) the Pharos lighthouse of Alexandria, (3) the Temple of Artemis at Ephesus, (4) the Colossus of Rhodes, (5) the Mausoleum of Halicarnassus, (6) the Statue of Zeus at Olympia, and (7) the Hanging Gardens of Babylon.

In the early 1900s A.D., the ancient city of Babylon was unearthed in present-day Iraq. There, amid the ruins of palaces and temples, was a strange, arched structure with a triple well. After the archaeologist carefully reread ancient accounts of the gardens (including the account by Herodotus) he concluded that the building housed the famous Hanging Gardens of Babylon.

Herodotus also wrote about the everyday lives of people in his time. He described the games they played with boards and dice and how soldiers prepared for battle (including how they wore their hair). These accounts give us insights we otherwise would never have had.

## Plato and Socrates

The Greek philosopher *Plato* wrote much of what we know today about his teacher, Socrates. Socrates was a philosopher in ancient Greece who taught his students to think by questioning them about ideas. The Athenian rulers thought that his popular teachings threatened their authority, so he was arrested, tried, and sentenced to death. To carry out the sentence, Socrates drank poison from the hemlock tree.

Though Socrates never wrote down his teachings, his pupil Plato wrote books as if they were conversations with his great teacher. Plato also wrote about utopia. Our word platonic comes from Plato's ideas about a perfect society.

Though most of Plato's writings are believed to be accurate and true, what he wrote about the island of Atlantis remains difficult for many to believe. Plato believed Atlantis was inhabited by an advanced society of people who were killed when the island was destroyed by a volcanic eruption. However, geologic evidence tells of a large volcanic eruption in the Mediterranean on the island of Santorini corresponding to the same time period discussed by Plato.

## Pliny

Another historian named *Pliny* wrote about the terrible eruption of Mt. Vesuvius, which destroyed the cities of Pompeii and Herculaneum in present-day Italy (it was under Roman rule at the time). Pliny was 17 years old when he wrote this eyewitness account from his home across the bay of Naples where the sun was obliterated from sight by the volcanic cloud that rose over 12 miles into the air:

> . . . *Then darkness fell as if a lamp had been turned out in a closed room. You could hear the screaming of women and children and the shouting of men— some were calling parents, others their wives or children and trying to recognize them in the dark by voice only. Some agonized over their own fate or that of their relatives, while others were terrified and prayed for death. Many asked the gods to help them, but more of them thought the gods were gone, and the universe had dropped into eternal darkness forever.*

30

Pliny's uncle was killed when he sailed across the bay to help friends near Pompeii. He suffocated from the sulfur fumes. Not only is Pliny's description of the various stages of the eruption considered to be accurate, it is miraculous that his written account has survived the centuries so that we may read it today.

Though Pliny's accuracy has been proven correct by scientific observations of other eruptions, other historic accounts must be examined carefully. Only when written sources are tested and proven can they be taken as fact. This is the reason archaeologists use artifacts and information from many different sources to paint a more complete and unbiased picture of the past.

## Activity: Make a Scroll and Be a Historian

### Materials
• Student Page 116

### Discussion

Discuss the kind of documents that might be most biased, like accounts of battles and descriptions of conquered people and their daily practices (religious and otherwise) by the conquerors.

Then discuss which documents would likely be most accurate. Some of the most accurate could be eyewitness accounts of catastrophic events (like Pliny's description of Mt. Vesuvius' eruption) and descriptions of everyday practices such as hair and clothing styles, games played, and rituals practiced. Descriptions of architectural marvels would likely be accurate if the writer described them from first-hand experience. For example, the Hanging Gardens of Babylon, which were considered one of the Seven Wonders of the Ancient World, were said to "appear suspended between heaven and earth." It is when second-hand information is written as fact that errors and bias occur.

Pliny writing his account of the eruption of Mt. Vesuvius, which destroyed the cities of Pompeii and Herculaneum.

31

Discuss elements of persuasive writing that are often found in biased material (such as radio and television advertisements): excessive use of adjectives (both positive and negative); use of insults and personal opinions; assertions that "smart" people use their product or idea; or using their product will make you popular and desirable. All of these ploys have been used by ancient writers just as they are used today.

**Student Page 116**

Students follow directions to make their own scrolls.
*(NOTE: It is best to do this activity in groups of two or three students.)*

Students complete one of these activities on their scrolls:
- Detail a sporting event (as if it were a battle) from a biased point of view.
- Report on important world or local events (catastrophic or otherwise).
- Describe the Seven Wonders of the Modern World (they could also describe seven architectural wonders of your area).
- Record "A Day in the Life of a Modern 6th–8th Grader" and specify hairstyles, clothes, food eaten, transportation, what school is like, how leisure time is spent, and so forth.

Students can read their historian's accounts to the class. Then host a class discussion on which accounts were biased and which were not.

**Challenge**

Some students may wish to write their historian's accounts using the Roman alphabet or even hieroglyphics. (See Chapter 3, Deciphering Ancient Writing, for specifics.)

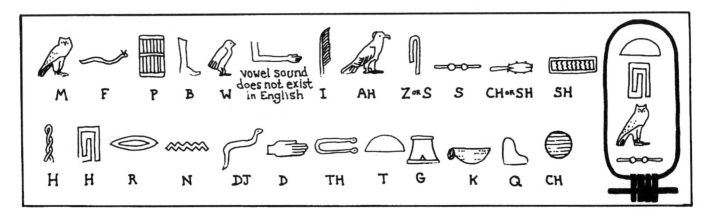

# Extensions

**Seven Wonders of the Ancient World Models**

Groups of students research one of the Seven Wonders of the Ancient World, construct a model of it, and then explain their model in an oral report to the class.

Lighthouse on Pharos Island, Alexandria, Egypt

**Atlantis**

Host a panel discussion on the existence or non-existence of the fabled city of Atlantis. Students should use information gleaned from recent research on the subject.

> *NOTE: Some scholars believe Atlantis to be the island of Santorini, or Thera as it was called in antiquity. The center of Santorini was blown away by a tremendous volcanic eruption. Others say Atlantis was the Minoan civilization on the island of Crete, which was destroyed by the great tidal wave created when Santorini's volcano exploded.*

33

# How Do We Know About the Past?

---

**Vocabulary:**

**fresco**—painting made on a freshly plastered wall
**frieze**—sculpture carved into a wall or building
**funerary objects**—items buried with the dead
**mosaic**—picture made from small pieces of rock or glass

---

## Chapter 5

## Learning from Ancient Art

Some objects of art give scholars a unique insight into ancient life by showing scenes of everyday life that would be impossible to interpret using artifacts, such as weapons, tools, or clothes, alone.

### From Cave Paintings to Frescoes

Early cave paintings in the Saharan desert have shown us that wildlife flourished in an area that is now a wasteland of sand. In the Lascaux cave in France, prehistoric humans painted detailed pictures of animals from the area that are now extinct. Clearly, these animals were important to our prehistoric ancestors. Not only were they important as a source of food, but the act of painting them may mean that these early humans performed rituals to ensure a good hunt.

Sahara cave paintings reveal a landscape supporting great animal and plant life—much different than the desert wasteland of today.

Lascaux Cave Paintings show the wealth of game in ancient Europe. The act of painting these prehistoric animals may have been part of an ancient hunting ritual.

34

An 8,000-year-old wall painting found in modern Turkey reveals a volcanic eruption and a town at the foot of the erupting mountain. No doubt the volcano played an important part in the lives of the townspeople.

This is the oldest depiction of an erupting volcano.
It was found on the wall of an ancient farming village in Turkey.

*Frescoes* were widely used throughout the Mediterranean civilizations. They have revealed much about the Minoan culture of Crete. For example, pictures of acrobats vaulting over the backs of bulls indicate the importance bulls played in this early culture.

The bull is an important symbol in Minoan culture.
The legend of the minotaur has its roots in Minoan culture.

In Egypt, frescoes line the walls of countless ancient tombs from floor to ceiling. These elaborate tomb paintings show the deceased person at work, at play, and with family at home. They have taught archaeologists a great deal about daily life in ancient Egypt.

35

## Funerary Objects

*Funerary objects* also provide archaeologists with a wealth of information. The items buried with the dead were for use in the afterlife. In ancient Egypt, these objects included models of people at work baking bread, making beer, and plowing fields. Again, these objects reveal significant information about everyday life in ancient Egypt.

Egyptian models like these were found in tombs and show countless scenes of everyday life.

The main reason that King Tutankhamen's royal tomb was such a major find was the wealth of funerary objects it contained. Until then, no royal Egyptian tomb had ever been found intact. All of them had been robbed at some point in the past.

The wealth of information and objects discovered in King Tut's tomb sheds light on royal burials in ancient Egypt. It remains the only royal tomb to be found intact by scholars.

*Archaeology*
Copyright ©1999 by Incentive Publications, Inc., Nashville, TN.

Viking burials usually included weapons, but no armor. When ivory carvings of Viking soldiers were found depicting a man in full armor on horseback, much was learned about that society.

When ivory carvings
such as this one were
discovered, a great
deal was learned about
Viking warriors.

## Pottery

Once it was learned that clay could be fashioned into shapes and fired in a kiln, artistry began. The Greeks, for example, painted elaborate scenes on their pottery.

Harvest scenes such as this one on a
Greek vase shed light on everyday life
in ancient times.

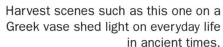

Native Americans on both continents—North America and South America—mastered the art of pottery. Pueblo pottery was decorated with striking clarity, and seems to have been ritually punctured. Even today, broken pieces of pottery can be found lying on the ground. For this reason, archaeologists have theorized that the pottery was ritually broken.

By carefully studying the figures on Pueblo pottery,
much is learned about ceremonial life as well as everyday life.

37

Much of what archaeologists know about ancient Chinese houses and architecture comes from models such as this one.

The Maya of present-day Mexico decorated their pottery with elaborate pictures and glyphs, some of which have yet to be deciphered. Ancient Peruvians also fashioned clay models of people playing instruments and engaging in other activities.

In ancient China, clay models of wooden houses have helped archaeologists understand what the houses of the early Chinese people looked like. This is especially helpful to scholars since all that remains of those houses today are their post-holes. Much of our knowledge of ancient China comes from models like the one pictured at left.

## Mosaics

*Mosaics* were common throughout the Roman empire. They, too, shed light on our understanding of ancient cultures. For example, mosaics in Pompeii illustrate the hairstyles and jewelry worn in the first century A.D.

A striking example of ancient art revealing important information is the Madaba Mosaic located in modern Jordan. The mosaic floor was discovered by accident when workmen were remodeling a church in the town of Madaba. What archaeologists found in the mosaic was the earliest known map of Jerusalem. It shows a colonnaded market that was previously unknown, and it provides clues to the layout of the ancient city that figures prominently in three of the world's religions—Judaism, Christianity, and Islam.

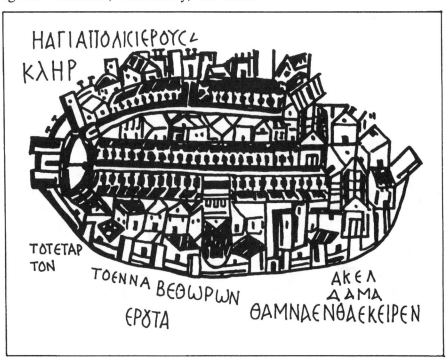

This mosaic, accidentally discovered in the Jordanian town of Madaba, is the earliest known map of Jerusalem.

38

## Friezes & Sculpture

Both *friezes* and sculpture are prevalent throughout the world's cultures and civilizations. The detail on them teaches us much about the past. For example, the Roman emperor Trajan had a frieze carved on a large marble column depicting scenes from his major military campaigns in Dacia.

Old sketches of the friezes and sculptures on the Parthenon in Athens help archaeologists understand their place and significance in restoring the site.

This is part of Trajan's frieze, which depicts the story of two wars he fought while commanding the Roman army. While marching from battle to battle, the soldiers constructed bridges and fortresses.

# Activity: Interpreting Ancient Art

### Materials
- Student Page 117

### Discussion

In pairs or small groups, students study the art objects and draw conclusions about the ancient cultures they represent. Encourage them to state obvious facts first, then infer further information.

Example:

The picture of the dolphin indicates close proximity to the ocean. The sea is of great importance to these people. It is a significant source of food and possible trade.

39

**Panel Discussion**

Once students have finished the assignment, hold a panel discussion with members of each group. Discuss the findings and conclusions of each group.

# Follow-Up Activity: Research Art from a Significant Culture

**Materials**
- Student Page 118

**Discussion**

Discuss and brainstorm to create a list of a number of ancient cultures students can research. These may include the ancient Egyptians, Greeks, Romans, Phoenicians, Vikings, Celts, Babylonians, Chinese, Indus Valley Civilization, or Aztec, Maya, Inca, or Hopewell Indians, and so forth.

**Student Page 118**

In pairs or small groups, students research a specific culture and draw (or trace) four significant pieces of art or artifacts representative of their culture, then write down the conclusions they can draw from them.

# Extension

**Research King Tut's Tomb**

Tell how it was discovered, what it contained, and why it is such an important find.

**Ancient Burial Rites**

Research and construct a model of an ancient burial. This can include Egyptian tombs and sarcophaguses, Neanderthal burials, Vikings in their long boats, mound burials in Britain, burial rites of the Etruscans, Scythians, Chinese, and so forth.

*NOTE: Refer to Chapter 18 for hands-on activities such*
*as making frescoes, mosaics, pottery, and models.*

# How Do We Know About the Past?

---

***Vocabulary:***

**Herculaneum**—Roman city destroyed in 79 A.D. by the volcanic eruption of Mt. Vesuvius

**Mt. Vesuvius**—volcano situated between the cities of Pompeii and Herculaneum which erupted in 79 A.D. and completely destroyed both cities

**Pompeii**—Roman city on the other side of Mt. Vesuvius from Herculaneum; also destroyed by Vesuvius' eruption

**Skara Brae**—small, ancient farming village in Scotland

---

## Chapter 6

### Time Capsules: Sites Frozen in Time

A site which is completely intact, one in which virtually nothing has been disturbed over time, is a rare archaeological find. These sites are usually buried quickly by natural disaster, such as a sandstorm, avalanche, or volcanic eruption. Because of the conditions of these catastrophic events, everything is covered and preserved. When the site is discovered and excavated, the state of preservation provides archaeologists with incredible amounts of information.

**Skara Brae**

*Skara Brae* was a small farming village situated beside a lake on the island of Orkney off Scotland. It consisted of about six stone houses, all connected by covered passageways. The people raised animals, farmed the land, and fished the lake for food. The settlement was abandoned about 2450 B.C. when a freak sandstorm engulfed everything.

Since timber was scarce so far north, everything, including the furnishings, were made of stone. Stone shelves were found along with beds, fireplaces, and even stone water tanks for keeping shellfish fresh for eating.

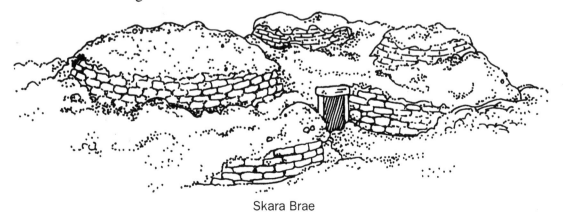

Skara Brae

41

*Archaeology*
Copyright ©1999 by Incentive Publications, Inc., Nashville, TN.

## Pompeii and Herculaneum

Almost 2,000 years ago, *Mt. Vesuvius* in southern Italy erupted and buried two cities, one on either side of the volcano. The entire event took less than 18 hours.

Mt. Vesuvius was situated between the cities of Pompeii and Herculaneum. When it erupted, it destroyed both cities in less than one day.

About noon on August 24, 79 A.D., Mt. Vesuvius erupted, sending an ash cloud 12 miles into the air. Because of the wind, the ash and pumice rained down on *Pompeii*, eventually burying it. *Herculaneum* was buried when a surge of deadly gas and lava flowed down the mountain.

Over the next several centuries, Vesuvius erupted several more times, continuing the layering of volcanic ash and rocks. Eventually, Herculaneum was covered by 65 feet of debris. Because of its location, Pompeii was only covered by twelve feet of ash and debris. As a result, Pompeii was easier to locate and excavate since its shallow layers were made mostly of compressed ash.

Pompeii's excavation began over 150 years ago. Herculaneum's began much later. Both cities have provided a unique look at Roman life 2,000 years ago. Homes of the rich and poor were preserved along with furniture, cooking pots, and other household items. Even a baby's wooden cradle was found with the baby's bones inside.

Thousands of people's bones were found in Pompeii. Over 100 years ago, the head archaeologist excavating the site realized that the ash covering Pompeii had hardened around the dead bodies of its inhabitants, leaving a hollow area in the ash. He poured plaster into these cavities. Once hardened and excavated, the plaster made a cast of each body. Casts were made of hundreds of people and animals, dramatically capturing the last moments of life in Pompeii.

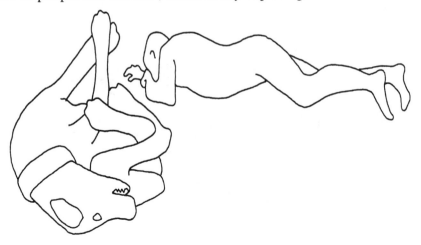

Plaster casts were made of people and even a dog as they lay in death—the result of Mt. Vesuvius' massive eruption

42

*Archaeology*
Copyright ©1999 by Incentive Publications, Inc., Nashville, TN.

The excavation of Herculaneum revealed very few human remains, so it was once thought that the people of Herculaneum somehow escaped before their town was buried. But, in 1982, a remarkable discovery changed that theory. Several skeletons were uncovered and a forensic archaeologist was called in to study the bones. Since Romans usually cremated their dead, these bones offered a unique chance to study the Romans themselves. The Pompeii bones had been encased in plaster over 100 years earlier because the detailed study of bones had not yet been developed.

Bones reveal much about people—their sex, age, health, diet, and the kind of work they did. And each Herculaneum skeleton had a story to tell. The tragedy of that day in August 79 A.D. became very real when the skeletons of a 14-year-old girl and a baby were found clinging to one another. From the expensive jewelry the baby wore, it surely came from a wealthy family. The 14-year-old girl, however, was not from a wealthy family. By the wear on her bones and teeth, it was determined that she had been starved or very ill when she was young and had done work too hard for her delicate body. She was probably a servant who was caring for the child.

The tangle of skeletons found huddled in storage caverns in the 1980s revealed a great deal about the lives of Herculaneum's citizens, as well as their tragic deaths.

This skull has a small plant sprouting from its eye socket where it lies with a mass of other human remains.

Another interesting fact about life in Pompeii and Herculaneum involves the many fast food shops available for people to eat their meals. These places existed because the average citizen lived in a small home with no kitchen. Only the wealthy, who could afford slaves and fuel, had kitchens.

**Other Discoveries**

Since the spectacular finds of Pompeii and Herculaneum were unearthed, other archaeological time capsules have been found around the world.

The remains of a Mayan village covered by a volcanic eruption was found in Central America. It is a significant find, revealing how the villagers lived, what they ate, and how they constructed their houses. Until this time capsule was found, most knowledge of the Mayan came only from the ruins of their stone temples. The humid climate had destroyed all other organic remains.

## Activity: A Site Frozen in Time

### Materials
- Student Page 119

### Discussion

Discuss with students the significant buildings and rooms in their lives—their bedrooms, history class, school cafeteria, stores in the mall, church sanctuaries, dance studios, and so forth—and the artifacts each contains. Then imagine a catastrophic event that would bury everything, such as an avalanche, rock slide, volcano, earthquake, or sandstorm. What would be left behind? Of the significant rooms and artifacts left behind, what would be revealed about: (1) the kind of site it was, (2) how the site was used, and (3) who used it?

### Student Page 119

Students fill out information, then map their significant room and all of its artifacts as they will be found when archaeologists excavate them. (Remember, a disaster causes buildings to collapse, and artifacts to scatter because of impact.) Students then number and label their artifacts on the map.

## Follow-Up Activity: Time Capsule Interpretation

### Materials
- Student Pages 119 and 120
- scissors
- ruler

### Discussion

When archaeologists excavate, they carefully map and record where all artifacts are located and when they were found. This is done with photography and by drawing the site, using a grid to properly record the size and juxtaposition of all items. Accuracy is extremely important, for if an artifact is found at one corner of the site, it can be interpreted differently than if it is situated elsewhere.

### Student Page 120

On the back of Student Page 119, students record their site number in code.

For example:

Judith Cochran's kitchen at 3613 Bell Court could become:

J C k 3613 B C

Students use scissors to cut Student Page 119 along the dotted line.

Individually, or in pairs, students exchange papers so that no one knows whose paper they have. Using information on Student Page 119, they complete the assignment on Student Page 120.

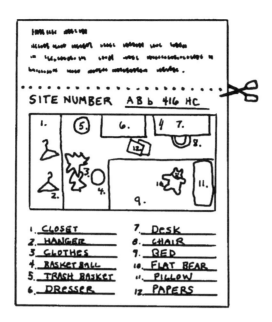

Using a ruler, students draw a grid on the original map of Student Page 119, similar to the grid on Student Page 120.

Use the grid to draw artifacts in exact places, then label them on the map. Once done, students answer the questions on the bottom of the page.

When Student Page 120 is complete, staple it to Student Page 119 and return them both to the original owner.

Students compare notes with the "archaeologist" who interpreted their paper.

As a class, share experiences regarding this assignment. Culminate the discussion by asking if it were difficult or easy to answer the questions interpreting the artifacts.

45

# What Is an Artifact?

## Chapter 7

## Material Remains

An artifact is any object made, modified, or used by humans. This includes the *lithics* left by early humans, as well as the animal bones left at their campsites.

The artifacts archaeologists find and use to interpret the past are usually objects that were lost, thrown away, or deliberately buried. (See Chapter 1, Aspects of Ancient Life through Artifacts.) Of these artifacts, very few survive due to the soil and weather conditions of the area and the material from which the object was made. *Organic* materials, such as plant and animal products, decay faster than *inorganic* materials, such as metal, stone, and pottery.

### Metals

It is usually an accident of nature that organic and many inorganic artifacts are preserved at all. Other than silver and gold, most metals deteriorate completely or corrode to such an extent that their original form becomes difficult to identify.

Iceman's ax, 5,500 years old

Although gold objects such as these earrings remain shiny and bright throughout time, objects such as the Iceman's copper ax would have deteriorated long ago had it not been for the unique conditions that preserved it.

## Organic Artifacts

Organic remains such as bone, wood, leather, and plant material *decompose* very quickly. In unique situations, however, they can be remarkably well preserved.

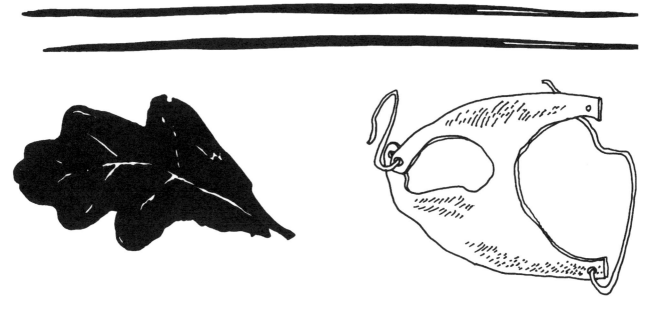

This oak leaf were excavated from the wreck of the ship *Mary Rose*.

This leather bikini is over 2000 years old. It was found in a well.

For example, 5,000-year-old clothing made of woven cotton from ancient Egypt has been preserved in tombs where it lay undisturbed in Egypt's hot, dry climate. This kind of find, however, is very rare.

## Pottery

Pottery is by far the most common artifact found in digs dating from 8,000 B.C. onward. This is because people in areas around the world began to fashion items from clay and fire them around 10,000 years ago. Though pottery is fragile and often breaks, the shards left behind remain virtually indestructible. Through the years, archaeologists have carefully recorded the different kinds of pottery objects made, when they were made, and by whom. As a result, when archaeologists excavate sites, they can look at the potsherds left behind and determine who lived in the area and when. By dating the pottery, all other artifacts found at the same level can be dated to the same time period.

# Activity: Which Artifacts Tell Your Story?

## Materials
• Student Page 121

## Discussion

Discuss artifacts the students have that will be left behind in 100 years for archaeologists to find. (List on board.)

47

*NOTE: Remind students that most organic artifacts will have decomposed in 100 years time. Then discuss artifacts their parents or grandparents might have. (List on board.)*

| Me | Parent/Grandparent |
|---|---|
| *examples may include:* | *examples may include:* |
| • a compact disk        • a set of chess pieces | • a hearing aid        • a television |
| • a candy wrapper       • a pair of tennis shoes | • coin money           • a letter opener |
| • a video game          • a computer | • a walking cane       • a gold ring |
| • a plastic necklace    • a hockey puck | • a picture frame      • a prescription bottle |
| • a ball-point pen      • a soda can | • a can of golf balls  • a pair of reading glasses |

Compare the artifacts of students with those of their parents and grandparents. How are they similar? How are they different? How could archaeologists differentiate between them in 100 years time?

**Student Page 121**

Students draw and label their own artifacts and those of a parent or grandparent. They then draw conclusions about the artifacts as an archaeologist.

Have students share the results with the class. Discuss how students' artifacts compare. For example: Would archaeologists be able to detect differences in taste and personality between one student and another? Why?

# Extension

**Materials**
   • a shoebox        • artifacts from home        • 5" x 7" index card

Students collect artifacts from home that reflect who they are and bring them to school in a shoebox. Students list contents of box on an index card and display their boxes of artifacts with the index card attached.

Identify student boxes with letters A, B, C, D, and so on. Have students then write their thoughts about the person each box represents. Share results with the class.

*NOTE: Students can later identify artifacts that will decompose over time.*

# Extension

Discuss pottery styles of today and determine what they would tell about our culture. Note similarities to (and differences from) ancient pottery.

48

# Where Artifacts Are Found

---

***Vocabulary:***

**tel**—artificial mountain made by layers of inhabitation over centuries

**stratified site**—place people have lived for hundreds or thousands of years and built settlements, one on top of the other

**domesticated animals**—tame animals that live with humans

**destruction layer**—layer of ruin caused by fire or natural disasters, such as earthquakes or volcanic activity

---

## Chapter 8

## How Artifacts Become Buried

### Catastrophic Events and Forces of Nature

With the exception of sites buried by catastrophic events like sandstorms, avalanches, or volcanic eruptions, the vast majority of sites have been buried slowly over time.

Any abandoned site will build up layers of dirt just as dust gathers in houses today. The forces of nature—wind and rain, flooding and drought—carry and distribute soil over sites as well. Even inhabited sites will have elevated floor levels because of dirt and mud brought in by people, animals, and all modes of transportation.

*Present-day ground level*

*Original ground level*

This site was used for a single period of time, then abandoned. Over time it has been covered with dirt.

## Tel Formations

The best way to illustrate how artifacts and building remains are buried is to explain an archaeological phenomenon known as a *tel* found in the Middle East. Even though countless sites throughout the world have built upon previous remains, the tel is the best example of the layering of one settlement on top of the next.

A water source is one of the basic criteria for founding any settlement. Since much of the Middle East is desert, there are fewer constant sources of water available. So where water was available, settlements were established from prehistoric times to present day.

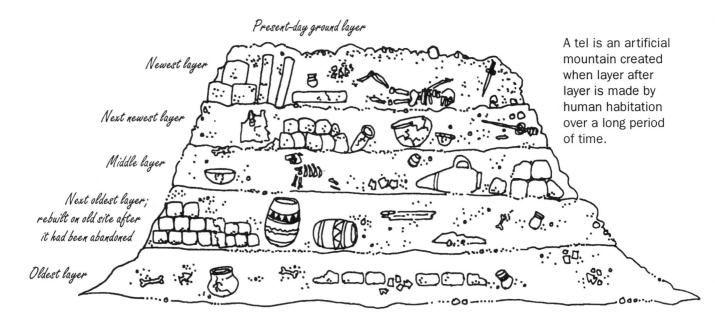

Present-day ground layer

Newest layer

Next newest layer

Middle layer

Next oldest layer; rebuilt on old site after it had been abandoned

Oldest layer

A tel is an artificial mountain created when layer after layer is made by human habitation over a long period of time.

## Jericho

The city of Jericho is an excellent example of a tel. Jericho is one of the earliest farming settlements in history. It is located at an oasis in the Jordan River Valley. Because of its warm climate and reliable water supply, people first settled there about 9,000 B.C. to raise crops and *domesticate* animals instead of relying on the nomadic life of hunting and gathering.

From an early farming settlement, Jericho gradually grew into a large and prosperous city. Trade with other cities around the Mediterranean gave Jericho great wealth. This probably explains the *destruction layers* found there because others wanted control of the lucrative trade. After each destruction, the city of Jericho was rebuilt. Each time, the new city was built on the ruins of the old one. Stone from ruined buildings was used to build new ones.

As layer upon layer is added to the settlement, the area becomes a *stratified site*, which archaeologists may excavate hundreds or thousands of years later.

## Oldest Artifacts Are the Deepest

Tels are only one manifestation of a stratified site, but all stratified sites began with the bottom layer first. So, the oldest artifacts are the deepest.

50

# Activity: My Stratified Life

### Materials
- Student Page 122

### Discussion

Discuss students' lives and the artifacts they used when they were babies (ages 0–5 years), when they started school (ages 5–10 years), and during the middle grades (ages 10–15). Talk about how their closets might be stratified if they had kept these artifacts, and how the oldest things would be the deepest in the closet.

### Student Page 122

Students draw and label artifacts from their lives at the appropriate layer. Have students share results with class. Attempt to interpret artifacts that reflect students' interests and personalities.

# Extension

### Stratified Collage

### Materials
- magazines or catalogs with lots of pictures
- 12" x 18" construction paper
- scissors
- glue or paste
- tracing paper

Students cut pictures from magazines or copy them onto tracing paper.

### Interview about Artifacts from a Decade

Discuss how the oldest artifacts are the deepest in stratified sites. Then compare this to students' own lives. Interview older people about significant artifacts from the 1950s, 1960s, 1970s, 1980s, and 1990s.

Construct a chart illustrating the artifacts from each decade in the appropriate placement (oldest, of course, being the deepest).

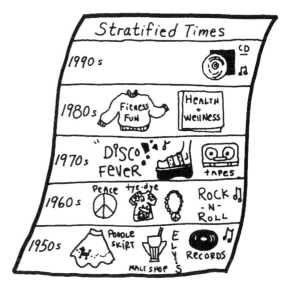

51

# Where Are the Artifacts Found?

---

**Vocabulary:**

**arid**—dry, parched

**carbonization**—the process of burning without oxygen, which leaves the artifact charred but intact

**coprolites**—preserved feces

**dendrochronology**—study of tree rings to date wooden remains

**marine archaeology**—excavations done on the ocean floor

**microorganisms**—small organisms, such as bacteria, that can be seen only through a microscope

**mummified**—corpse preserved by embalming or drying

**textiles**—woven or knitted fabric

---

## Chapter 9

## How Artifacts Are Preserved

The fact that artifacts from the past are preserved at all is miraculous. Most items decay over time. Fortunately there are extreme conditions that preserve some objects from the past. Dry climates, whether they are hot or cold, preserve artifacts because the microorganisms that cause decomposition cannot live in cold, dry, or airless conditions. Ice also has preserved some spectacular finds. Water, whether it is saltwater or fresh, can also halt the destruction of artifacts under the right conditions.

### Hot or Cold, Dry and Airless

Deserts around the world have preserved many organic materials like food, grains, baskets, sandals, plants, and textiles. The high and dry regions of Peru have produced the *mummified* remains of people buried thousands of years ago. In fact, Peruvian mummies predate those found in Egypt. Unlike the ancient Egyptians, ancient Peruvians did not process the corpses of their dead to mummify the remains. This mummification was caused by the cold, *arid* climate, and, in some cases, as the result of an earthquake.

*Archaeology*
Copyright ©1999 by Incentive Publications, Inc., Nashville, TN.

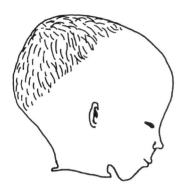

Peruvian child naturally
mummified in an earthquake.

Egyptian mummy wrapped and processed
by embalming to preserve the remains.

Rope sandals and wood hundreds of years old have been found in the hot, dry climate of the American southwest. Pueblo settlements were built into the cliffs and plains of the region. *Dendrochronology* was pioneered at these pueblos in the 1920s and allowed scientists to precisely date the wood remains. This aided in the reconstruction of history at the pueblos.

Cliff Palace pueblo at Mesa Verde has many preserved organic remains such as sandals, wood, and coprolites. In the 1920s, dendrochronology was pioneered at this site, and it has proven to be quite accurate.

Wooden remains and other items such as brooms and brushes have also been found intact in the hot and dry deserts of both Egypt and China.

Airless environments completely preserve items. Such is the case with the volcanic eruption of Mt. Vesuvius, which buried the towns of Pompeii and Herculaneum under heavy layers of volcanic ash. Even bread was *carbonized* and is still recognizable today, complete with its baker's stamp.

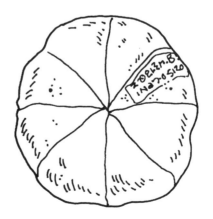

Carbonized bread complete with
baker's stamp from Pompeii.

53

## Ice

Frozen tombs in Siberia, Russia, have yielded an array of artifacts that would have decayed long ago. Though the tombs were robbed soon after burial, water had seeped in and frozen everything, thus preserving them. Tattoos were found on the bodies of the buried chiefs along with saddles and horses. Leather flasks made from leopard skin, horn carvings, and detailed embroidery reveal a complex society with expert craftsmen.

The tombs were underground log-built chambers and were decorated like houses, complete with wall hangings, pots, carpets, and furniture.

Siberian tombs were decorated like houses with carpets, pots, furniture, and clothes.

## The Iceman

A recent find preserved in ice is the body of a man found by hikers in the Alps in 1991. At first, the body was thought to be a recent murder victim. Then it became clear that the body was over 5,000 years old! Over the years, the ice had mummified the body and kept the artifacts in perfect shape. The iceman, too, had tattoos. He also carried several tools, food in his backpack, and a leather pouch worn much like the fanny packs of today.

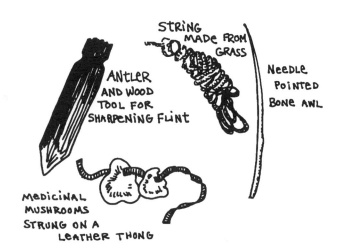

The Iceman's leather pouch contained a needle-pointed bone awl, grass string, antler and wood tool for sharpening flint, and medicinal mushrooms strung on a leather thong.

## Water: Saltwater and Fresh

Countless shipwrecks litter the bottoms of the seas of the world. As long as people have lived beside bodies of water, they have fashioned boats to traverse them. Eventually, trade developed, along with war to control the trade, and boats were an integral part of it all.

Under the sea, artifacts are attacked by marine organisms, salt, and swift currents. However, once the remains have settled on the ocean floor and are covered with silt, they are preserved.

Such was the case of England's King Henry VIII's flagship, the Mary Rose. It was sunk in a battle off the coast of England in 1545. When it was excavated from the silt that covered it, many remarkable artifacts were found. Leather shoes, some still on the feet of skeletons, and woolen stockings along with silk, satin, and lace all survived. Arrows were the consistency of soft butter when excavated, so great care was taken in preserving them.

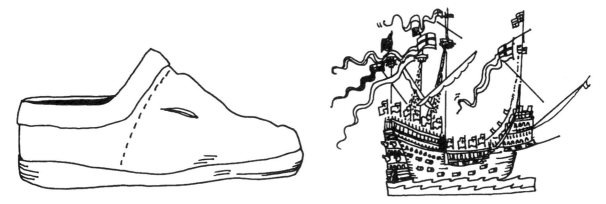

Because of the conditions underwater, most of the artifacts on board the Mary Rose (right) were preserved, including leather shoes and even woolen socks.

Freshwater peat bogs and fens (or marshes) like those in Britain also preserve what was thrown into them because decay-causing bacteria have no oxygen to survive. Besides wood, leather, and metal artifacts, bogs have yielded well-preserved bodies. Most appear to have been sacrificed in religious ceremonies. One was strangled, hit on the head with a blunt object, had his throat cut, and then was laid naked in a boggy pool. Much was learned about the life of the man—his smooth fingernails were not worn by manual labor, his bones revealed his age and any ailments he may have had, and the contents of his stomach revealed his diet.

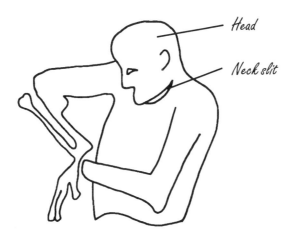

From the many artifacts found in marshes and bogs, archaeologists believe the articles may have been sacrifices to the gods.

Wells have also yielded interesting artifacts. In Mexico at the ancient Mayan city of Chichen Itza, a sacred well held over 6,000 items, including jade, gold, copper, incense, and the bones of sacrificial victims. Obviously, the well had religious significance to the Maya.

**Coprolites, Ghost Ships, and Humidity**

Unusual items of interest to archaeologists are *coprolites* and ancient toilets. Much can be learned about the health and diet of ancient people from these things. For example, it has been discovered that ancient Egyptians suffered from intestinal worms.

Sometimes archaeologists can learn much from something that has already decayed and disappeared. In Sutton Hoo in England, the ghost impression of a 90-foot long ship was found in a mound. All the timbers had rotted away in the acidic soil, leaving a hard crust in the sand and the iron fittings that had held the timbers together. Still, by careful excavation a great deal was learned about the boat's size and construction.

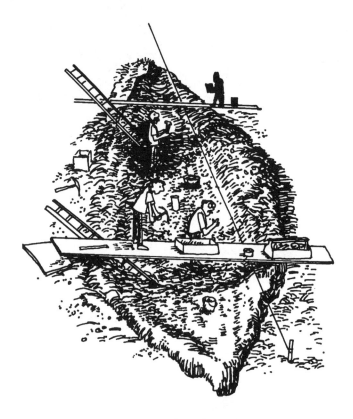

Ship Shape
In the 1930s, excavations at the
mounds of Sutton Hoo unearthed the
distinctive shape of a large ship. The
acid soil had deteriorated everything
except the iron rivets that once held the
timber frame together. Only a hard,
sandy crust revealed where wooden
planks once existed.

In humid environments organic artifacts decompose quickly, leaving only stone and pottery behind. That is why our knowledge of cultures living in jungles and tropical rain forests is limited to what we can learn from their stone temples, tools, and buildings.

# Activity: How Artifacts Are Preserved

## Materials

- Student Page 123
- 35 clear plastic cups (approx. 8 oz)
- 35 pieces of fruit (apples work well)
- plastic wrap
- pottery clay (approx. 5 lb.)
- pea gravel or coarse sand (approximately 10–12 cups)
- masking tape
- rubber bands
- lamp
- freezer
- refrigerator

## Student Page 123

This experiment replicates the various conditions in which artifacts are found—dry, frozen, humid, underwater uncovered, and underwater covered.

1. Divide students into seven groups of five students each. Each group receives the following materials:
   - 5 clear plastic cups
   - 5 pieces of fruit
   - plastic wrap
   - enough pottery clay to completely cover one piece of fruit
   - 1½ cups pea gravel or coarse sand
   - masking tape
   - rubber bands

2. Students label cups with masking tape as follows: Dry, Humid, Frozen, Underwater and Uncovered, Underwater and Covered.

3. Set up each cup according to these directions:

   **Dry:** Fill ⅓ of cup with gravel. Place fruit in the gravel so it still can be seen. Place under a lamp to recreate the hot, dry conditions in which some artifacts are found.

   **Humid:** Fill ⅓ of cup with gravel. Place fruit on top of gravel. Add water until it just touches fruit. Cover with plastic wrap and seal with rubber bands. Store in a place where it will stay at room temperature.

   **Frozen:** Fill ⅓ of cup with gravel. Place fruit into gravel, then pour in more gravel until fruit is covered, but can be seen through the cup. Fill cup with water and place in a freezer.

57

**Underwater and Uncovered:** Follow directions for Frozen cup, but place in a refrigerator.

**Underwater and Covered:** Surround fruit with damp clay and press until it is airtight (do this with plastic wrap so your hands don't get dirty). Fill 1/3 of cup with gravel and fill with water until it just begins to show on top of gravel. Place clay covered fruit on gravel. Cover cup with plastic wrap and seal with rubber bands. Store in a refrigerator.

Once a week for four weeks, students gather their cups together and record their observations on Student Page 124. They then replace the cups in their appropriate places until the next week.

## Student Page 124

Students follow directions and record their observations of the fruit in each cup once a week for four weeks. At the end of the fourth week, students write their conclusions about the conditions in which organic artifacts are preserved.

Below is the list of the conditions and the results of this experiment:

| *Condition* | *Result* |
|---|---|
| 1. Dry (like the Dead Sea Scrolls and the mummies in Egypt and Peru) | Artifact shrivels up |
| 2. Humid (like the SE Asian temples and the Mayan sites in Mexico and Central America) | Artifact rots and smells |
| 3. Frozen (like the Ice Man found in the Alps and the Siberian burials) | Artifact remains the same |
| 4. Underwater and Uncovered (like most shipwrecks) | Artifact rots |
| 5. Underwater and Covered (like the bogman and the Mary Rose) | Artifact remains almost the same |

58

# Artifacts — Teacher's Manual

# What Artifacts Reveal

**Vocabulary:**

**amphora**—round-bottomed pottery jar for storing liquids

**ceramic technologist**—specialist who studies all aspects of how and where ancient pottery was made

**diagnostics**—pieces of pottery used for analysis, including rims, collar, handle, base, and potter's marks

**firing**—baking pottery in a kiln

**kiln**—oven where pottery is heated to very high temperatures

**pithoi**—extremely large, heavy clay jars used to store grain and other food stuffs

**pottery terminology:** . . . . . . . . . . . . rim

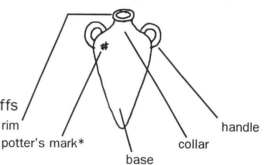

potter's mark*     collar     base     handle

*mark on pot indicating who made it

## Chapter 10

### Pottery Speaks

Pottery reveals a great deal about the people who made it. Because it does not decay easily, archaeologists find lots of potsherds at sites. By analyzing the shape of the pot, how it was made, and the minerals in the clay, archaeologists can determine where the clay came from, where it was made, and how it was made.

**Where and How Pots Were Made**

Pottery was first made in the Middle East about 10,000 years ago. Some people used the "coil method" by rolling the clay into long coils, spiraling the coils into the shape of a pot, then smoothing down the sides. Later, potters used a wheel, which they turned with either their hands or their feet. Pots made on a wheel had a more uniform shape.

Pots were first dried, then heated over an open fire to harden. Later, *kilns* were constructed to achieve higher temperatures and to create harder, more durable pots.

Pots made by both the coil and wheel methods

*Archaeology*
Copyright ©1999 by Incentive Publications, Inc., Nashville, TN.

## Diagnostics

Since so many pieces of broken pottery are found at virtually any site, archaeologists keep only the pieces that tell the most about the pots: rims, collars, handles, bases, and potter's marks.

Rims and collars reveal how large the pot was by measuring it on a diameter scale. The thickness of the walls evident in these diagnostic pieces also provides a clue as to how large the overall piece was. Handles also give clues as to the size of the pot since only a large, thick handle could support a large pot. Bases also reveal the size and use of the pot.

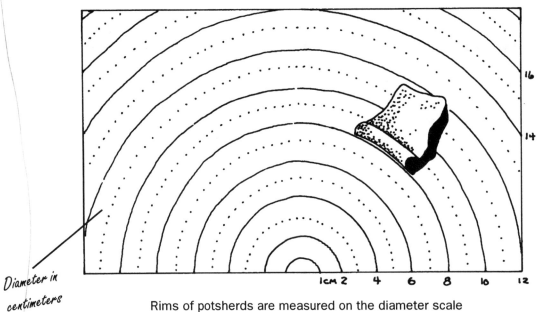

*Diameter in centimeters*

Rims of potsherds are measured on the diameter scale
to determine the size of the pot's opening and its approximate size.

Potter's marks help archaeologists understand where the pottery came from. Was it imported from a distance or made locally? If locally made, how many potters were working in the area? Answers to these questions can indicate trade with other settlements and also the local population in ancient times. Several local potters would mean there was a community large enough to support them, or that pots were made for trading purposes.

Pots are drawn to scale with half of the drawing showing the outside and the other half showing the inside wall of the pot.

60

*Archaeology*
Copyright ©1999 by Incentive Publications, Inc., Nashville, TN.

When analyzing pots, *ceramic technologists* draw cross-sections of the entire pot. This allows them to see both the outside and its markings as well as the inside. It also reveals the construction of the walls and how they were fired.

Further analysis of the clay is done by ceramic technologists who examine thin cross-sections of the pottery under a microscope to determine the minerals present. Once the mineral content is known, the technologist can locate where the clay came from. This, too, gives a good idea of whether the clay was imported or local.

In ancient times, most pottery was produced by local potters using local clay. Later, more pottery was imported and exported along established trade routes.

Different colors in the sample under the microscope
reveal the various minerals in the clay.

**Types of Pots**

When pottery was first being made some 10,000 years ago, the shapes were small and crude. Later, larger and more uniform shapes were made to serve specific purposes. Cooking pots were made from rough, strong clay so that they wouldn't crack when heated. *Amphora* are large round-bottomed jars once used throughout the Mediterranean to hold wine and other liquids. In fact, taverns in Pompeii had counters with holes in them to hold amphora filled with various liquids.

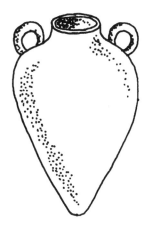

61

*Pithoi* were large jars weighing hundreds of pounds. They were used to store dry goods such as grain.

"Pithos" are large store jars taller than a person. This example is from Knossos on Crete.

Archaeologists who are ceramic experts can look at broken pieces of pottery and determine:
   (1)  the kind of pot it was
   (2)  its purpose
   (3)  when it was made in antiquity

Dating pottery is one of the major methods archaeologists employ to date their sites.

This thin, delicate bowl could be used only for
special occasions, as it was not practical for daily use.
This is Nabataean from the city of Petra in Jordan.

This German pot was most likely used for cooking. The
simple design and rough clay make it suitable for daily use.

 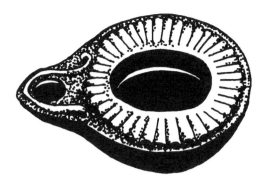

These lamp styles differ greatly even though their age is only about 50 years apart.

## Activity: Modern-Day Equivalent

### Materials
• Student Pages 125, 126, and 127

### Discussion

Discuss how pottery was the only container in which to store liquids and dry goods. There were no boxes or plastic bags.

Brainstorm about what the modern-day equivalents of amphora and pithoi might be, and what kinds of things would be stored in them today.

### Student Page 125

Students write modern items they would store in amphora and pithoi in ancient times.

### Student Pages 126 and 127

Students bring in rims of broken flower pots, plates, cups, and so forth, and measure their diameters using the diameter scales.

## Extension

Students draw cross-sections of modern pottery items, such as cups, plates, bowls, mugs, and so forth.

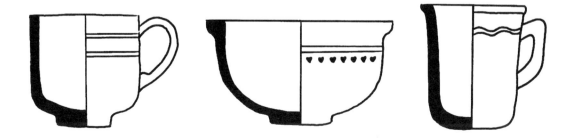

63

# Getting Ready to Dig

---

**Vocabulary:**

**minaret**—slender tower on a mosque from which a man—the muezzin—calls Moslems to prayer

**mosque**—Moslem place of worship

**muezzin**—crier calling Moslems to prayer from a mosque's minaret

**sieve**—wire mesh used to sift excavated dirt to recover small artifacts such as beads

**trowel**—small hand shovel; most commonly used archaeological tool

**balk**—wall of a square being excavated

---

## Chapter 11

### Tools, Customs, and Daily Schedule

**Tools**

The most common tools archaeologists use are the hand *trowel*, hand pick, brush, dental tools (for delicate work), and *sieves*. Excavating is very hard work, no matter what the climate is or what part of the world the site is in. It takes muscle to move the dirt and find what is buried there.

Cameras to photograph squares and a pencil and paper to draw and record daily progress are also of importance.

Measuring tape is used to plan and lay out squares on the site. It is also used when drawing balks.

Small brushes are used to sweep dirt from delicate artifacts.

This scale stick is used when photographing artifacts to indicate their size.

This ordinary bricklayer's trowel is an archaeologist's main tool.

Hand picks loosen hard-packed dirt.

Dental picks are used for careful work on delicate artifacts.

*Archaeology*
Copyright ©1999 by Incentive Publications, Inc., Nashville, TN.

## Customs and Food

Depending on the country where the site is located, archaeologists must be sensitive to the local customs. For example, when excavating in the Moslem countries of the Middle East, both women and men must keep their arms and legs covered at all times. Often, women must keep their hair covered as well, as Moslem culture dictates. From *minarets*, *muezzins* issue a call to prayer five times daily, so excavators in the Middle East should expect to hear that. In Moslem countries the holy day is Friday, so stores and restaurants are usually closed that day.

In Israel, the holy day is Saturday, and local customs are more similar to those in the United States. Both Jewish and Moslem traditions forbid the eating of pork, so it is not readily available in the Middle East. Foods that are available are: humus (garbanzo bean paste), falafel (fried balls of garbanzo bean paste put in pita bread), and schwarma (thin slices of lamb rolled in pita bread).

## Daily Schedule

Though daily schedules vary from site to site, the one below depicts an average day on the average dig.

| | |
|---|---|
| 4:30 A.M | Wake up |
| 5:00–5:30 | First breakfast |
| 5:30 | Go to site, begin digging |
| 7:30–7:45 | Break |
| 9:00–9:30 | Second breakfast |
| 10:30–10:45 | Break |
| 12:30 P.M. | Return to camp and clean up for main meal |
| 1:00 | Lunch (main meal of day) |
| 2:00–4:00 | Quiet time |
| 4:00–6:00 | Pottery washing; lab work (cataloguing artifacts, numbering potsherds); specialists work on artifacts |
| 6:00 | Dinner |
| 7:00–9:00 | Class, lecture or free time |
| 9:00 | Lights out |

Throughout the world, except in a few countries like the United States, a two-hour break is taken at midday, about lunchtime. This allows people to eat, relax, and avoid working during the hottest part of the day. Later, they return to work refreshed and rested for the remainder of the day.

# Activity: Schedule Comparisons

### Materials
- Student Page 128

### Discussion
Discuss similarities and differences between the archaeological schedule and students' own schedules. Also discuss other comparisons of diet and dress.

### Student Page 128
Students cite similarities and differences between their own daily routines and the example given of schedule, food, and dress of an archaeological dig in Jordan or other Moslem countries in the Middle East.

# Extensions

### Archaeological Tool Display
Collect all of the tools archaeologists use to excavate. Arrange and label them with a description of how they are used. Take instant snapshots of students using the tools on their own dig (use with Chapter 18, Hands-On Approach to Archaeology).

### Research Countries and Sites

### Materials
- travel brochures about various countries
- In Situ newsletter from Jordan (Student Page 129)
- sample list of sites (Student Page 130)

Students research the customs, sites, and other specifics of a chosen country and dig they would like to visit. After researching everything, students pack a suitcase (one only) with all they will need for a six-week dig.

# Where and How to Dig

**Vocabulary:**

**aerial photography**—photographing an area from the air to detect features

**architecture**—style or method of constructing buildings

**features**—permanent fixtures of a site such as postholes or cooking pits

**field**—a section or area of a site to be excavated

**ground penetrating radar (GPR)**—radar signals sent into an area to detect underground features

**infrared photography**—type of photography that detects temperature changes caused by buried features

**square**—sites are divided and excavated in squares (usually 5- to 8-foot squares)

**survey**—general review of an area for archaeological features

**test trench**—narrow strip excavated to see if artifacts are present

## Chapter 12

## Surveying and Digging

### Surveying Area

Before archaeologists can begin digging, they must know where to dig. This is determined by a *survey* of the area. Surveys look for both artifacts and features. They are done a number of ways: searching for surface artifacts and building remains, using *aerial photography*, and sending out *ground penetrating radar.*

### Surface Artifacts and Building Remains

Just by walking around an area, artifacts such as broken pottery and the stone walls of ancient settlements can be found. By recognizing the kind of pottery and when it was made, archaeologists get an idea about when a settlement was built. Though stone walls were often built in ancient times, it is only when the pottery and other artifacts around it are dated that the age of the wall can be determined.

Surface pottery sherds indicate where and when people lived in an area.

*Archaeology*
Copyright ©1999 by Incentive Publications, Inc., Nashville, TN.

When a building's style of *architecture* can be identified, it also helps date the site.

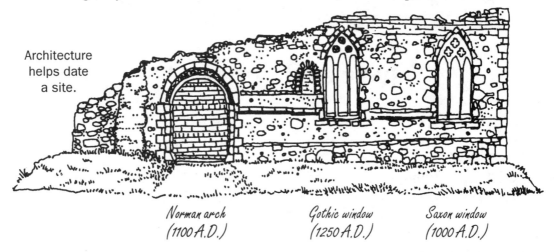

Architecture helps date a site.

*Norman arch*
*(1100 A.D.)*

*Gothic window*
*(1250 A.D.)*

*Saxon window*
*(1000 A.D.)*

Sometimes, farmers plowing their fields will turn up ancient building stones or other artifacts purely by accident. This will lead archaeological survey teams to dig a *test trench* in hopes of finding other artifacts that will identify the kind of site it might be: Roman outpost, burial tomb, early human settlement, or so forth.

Digging a test trench helps archaeologists identify the type of site it is.

### Aerial Photography

Aerial photography and infrared photography can reveal features not visible on the ground. Crops grow differently over various underground features, and these subtle differences can be detected with aerial photography. Other features cause temperature changes over the *field* that can be detected by *infrared photography*.

Infra-red photography is sensitive to temperature changes on the ground.

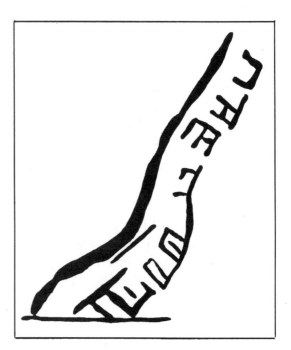

Crop marks are visible from the air. These differences in crop growth are caused by buried ditches and walls.

68

## Ground Penetrating Radar

Various machines passed over the ground can defect features buried deeper than those seen in aerial photography. Things like stone walls and tombs reflect signals much like airplanes do on traditional radar screens. However, there is much more interference in the ground than in the air. Large rocks for example, can cause confusing readings, as can soils high in mineral content. Therefore, ground penetrating radar (GPR) results are analyzed very carefully before drawing any conclusions.

The GPR unit is rolled over an area in a grid pattern to detect any underground structures such as this buried Etruscan tomb.

Other radar detection is done with sophisticated satellite radar revealing features below the ground surface that would be impossible to detect otherwise. In fact, space shuttle astronauts have taken pictures for archaeologists. This technique is very helpful when used on large sites with many possible places to dig.

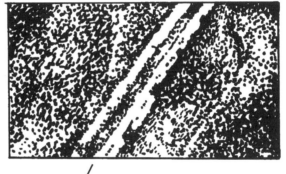

This satellite image of the Great Wall of China reveals the remains of a second, earlier wall.

*Two lines of Great Wall reveal an earlier buried structure.*

## Digging

Once the survey results are in, the archaeologist must decide where to start digging on the site. This is a major decision to make. Archaeologists have been known to dig for an entire season on a site and find nothing because the wrong *squares* were excavated. All archaeologists can do is make their best educated guess given all the information gathered from the survey.

The site is mapped out in a grid to establish areas or fields with squares in them. This is usually done with stakes and string. Once the squares are set up, the digging begins. Each site is given a number, as is each square and each layer in that square as it is found.

Volunteers open up this square by first removing the layer of topsoil.

69

*Archaeology*
Copyright ©1999 by Incentive Publications, Inc., Nashville, TN.

If a site were used only once, artifacts are found in a shallow layer just below the topsoil. In this case, the area is cleared of the topsoil to make the features visible. If postholes were dug, they will leave darkened circles in the soil. Once all the postholes are visible, the archaeologists will study and measure them to determine the shape of the structures.

If a site has been used for a short time, the area is often cleared to reveal the features as well as the artifacts.

If a site were used over a long period of time, there will be layers of artifacts and *features*. This layering is called stratification.

As each square is dug, or excavated, all artifacts that are found are put in plastic bags or buckets (depending on their size). Each bag or bucket will be tagged to indicate the specific site and square it came from (including which layer, if the square is stratified).

Often the dirt is sifted to search for small artifacts. Seals, small bones, beads, and other jewelry are often found this way. They, too, are tagged properly with their locus.

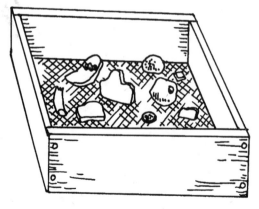

Artifacts are recovered
by sifting excavated dirt.

Small fragile artifacts are placed into
plastic bags along with a locus sheet.

70

# Activity: Where Would You Dig and Why?

**Materials**
- Student Page 131

**Discussion**

Organize students into pairs or small groups. Discuss the features in each site on Student Page 134 and what each one might be. (Remember, archaeologists are learning about everyday life in ancient times, so they aren't looking for gold.) Have students offer systematic ways to excavate each site.

Archaeologists are making these kinds of decisions all the time, based on precisely the same information the students have. An educated guess is the best they can do.

**Student Page 131**

In pairs or small groups, students decide which two squares to open at each site. Once done, groups share their decisions and tell why they made them. (Teacher shares articles found at each site.)

> *NOTE: In the GPR (ground penetrating radar) image, the white areas reflect the highest intensity of underground structures. The black areas have the lowest intensity. Therefore, the white areas seem to reveal parallel walls with rooms between them (these are often called casemate walls) and may resemble the drawing below.*

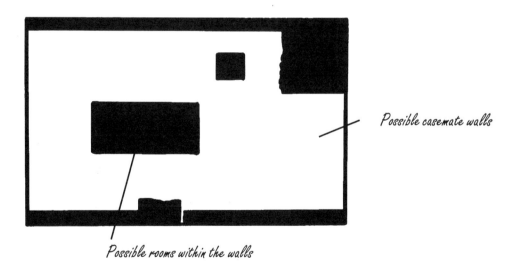

*Possible casemate walls*

*Possible rooms within the walls*

71

# Recording Progress

**Vocabulary:**
  **balk**—wall of a square being excavated
  **generation**—a span of approximately 20 years
  **methodology**—methods used to excavate and interpret finds

## Chapter 13

## Stratigraphy and Field Notes

It is a sad fact that by excavating a site, the site is destroyed. All the artifacts are removed, and all that is left is a hole in the ground. That is why it is so important to meticulously record everything while excavating so that future archaeologists can review the records and analyze the results. Perhaps future archaeologists can apply revolutionary new techniques to the data and answer long-standing questions or reinterpret findings.

In fact, whenever prehistoric cave sites are studied today, only half or a third of the site is excavated. This is so there will be enough left for future archaeologists with better methodology to apply new knowledge to the site.

### Stratigraphy

As discussed earlier, the longer a site has been inhabited, the more layers or stratification there will be. When excavating, it is very important that each layer be identified and dated, for each has a story to tell about a particular time of the site.

The types of artifacts found in each layer and the consistency of each layer tells archaeologists a great deal. For example, if a layer is nothing but ash and charcoal, it can indicate a mass destruction by fire. Or, if one layer dates to 100 years earlier than the next, it can indicate the site was abandoned for several generations before being inhabited again.

*This layer dates to 125 years later than the destruction layer. The site was abandoned for that period of time.*

*Destruction layer of ash and charred remains*

*Archaeology*
Copyright ©1999 by Incentive Publications, Inc., Nashville, TN.

When such destruction or abandonment of a site is evident, archaeologists are left wondering why the site was abandoned. Was there a war, disease, or crop failure? Did the water supply give out? Did trade routes change? So many questions are left for future archaeologists to answer with new archaeological techniques. Meanwhile, nothing replaces good excavation, documentation, and field notes.

## Field Notes

While excavating, archaeologists photograph, map, and draw the floor of their square and each *balk* (or wall) often. This details not only the artifacts and features uncovered, but also records the day-to-day progress of the dig.

Each layer, or strata, is identified with a label.

This archaeologist draws the balk after it is photographed. Every day he details every aspect of his square to scale, including the floor and each of the four sides.

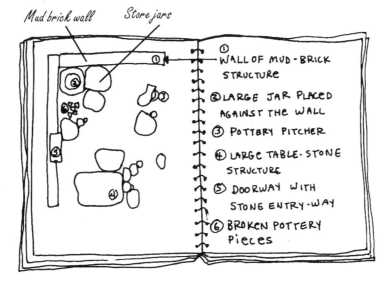

Notebook of the site contains carefully labeled drawings.

Field notes record information pictorially and in written form. Meticulous record-keeping is essential in archaeology.

73

# Activity: Field Notes from a Tel in Jordan

### Materials
- Student Page 132

### Discussion

Discuss the specific items in the balk drawings and floor map. Remind students that large collared pithoi are used for storage and a casemate wall is used to fortify and protect the settlement.

### Student Page 132

In pairs, students interpret the field notes and record questions this data raises. (Archaeologists at this site in Jordan want to know how such a fortified site was attacked and subsequently burned.)

*NOTE: This page can also be used with Chapter 15 (Context, Scientific Procedures, and Evolution of Objects) to discuss what dating tests students would use on these artifacts.*

## Stratigraphy Activity and Explanation/Interpretation

### Materials
- Student Pages 133 and 134
- clear plastic 1- or 2-liter bottles (one per each pair of students)
- several different colors of fish tank gravel
- artifacts that are datable and undatable (e.g., coins, bottle openers, pop-tops, pull tabs, popsicle sticks, shoestrings, paper clips, and so forth)
- thin-line permanent marking pens
- rulers
- scissors
- dirt
- sand
- ash

Each pair of students layers their plastic bottle with at least three layers of different colored material and places artifacts so that they are visible from the outside in each appropriate layer.

*NOTE: Remind students that the bottom layer is the oldest. Also, if they want to represent a destruction layer, they can use charred wood as well as ash.*

Encourage students to make variations in the configuration and thickness of each layer.

74

Students circle "Explanation" and proceed to draw and describe each artifact, then explain the story of the stratified site they have constructed.

Once their stratified site is done, it is given to another pair of students to draw and interpret the site on Student Pages 133 and 134.

Students use rulers and thin-line permanent markers to draw a one-inch grid around the plastic bottle.

**Student Page 133**

Students draw their stratified site to scale, then label and describe the material in each layer.

**Student Page 134**

Students circle "Interpretation," then proceed to draw and label the artifacts in each layer. They then date each layer using information gleaned from the artifacts.

Students write an interpretation of the site and report findings to the class. Encourage pairs to compare their interpretation with the "Description" of the pair who constructed the site. Discuss reasons the "Descriptions" and "Interpretations" vary significantly.

Remind students that artifacts are all archaeologists have to reconstruct the past, and that the majority of artifacts excavated were either lost or thrown away items. This fact can limit the interpretation of a site.

*Archaeology*
Copyright ©1999 by Incentive Publications, Inc., Nashville, TN.

# Underwater Archaeology

## Chapter 14

## Finding and Excavating Shipwrecks

Marine archaeology is a relative newcomer to the field of archaeology, and it has some challenging aspects to it. The tools used for underwater excavation are quite different from those used for land excavation, and record-keeping has required some unique measures. Marine archaeology is also much more expensive than a traditional dig because of the specialized equipment.

### Finding Sunken Ships

Often historical records are consulted to get as much information about a specific ship as possible. Historical accounts are read and carefully analyzed to narrow the area of ocean to search. Even though the area has been narrowed down, the process of surveying the ocean bottom is a long and tedious one.

Sonar bounces sound waves off the sea bottom and registers objects as they reflect the waves back. This sonar image is the side view of a ship that is over 340 feet beneath arctic ice.

Archaeologists drag a *sonar* device behind the vessel as it sails back and forth to cover an entire area. Sonar works like radar, but uses sound waves instead of radio waves. The sound waves bounce off objects underwater and are reflected back to the ship. Reading the echoes that bounce back indicate the size, type, and shape of an object below. Most all major shipwrecks have been found this way.

Once a wreck has been found, small unmanned submarines equipped with video equipment can be sent to explore the wreck site. These are often used at depths too great for divers to go. The *Titanic* was discovered and explored in this way.

## Beginning the Excavation

As with any archaeological site, the area must be divided into squares. This is done using plastic pipe joined together over the site in a grid pattern. Each square is numbered, and then the excavation begins.

Divers uncover artifacts by carefully waving silt away with their hands, putting the silt in buckets, or using an *air lift*. An air lift works like a giant vacuum hose that sucks up the silt and feeds it through a wire mesh sifter on board ship. It is the best way to recover small artifacts. Divers must be careful not to stir up too much silt as they work or it will cloud the area, making visibility poor. If this happens, all divers can do is wait for it to settle before continuing.

Since divers are limited to two 20-minute dives daily, so they must make good use of their time underwater and should be careful not to disturb the area.

## Recovering Artifacts

To recover a large, heavy object, bags are attached to the object and filled with air from extra air tanks. The objects then float to the surface where crew on board the ship will recover them.

All artifacts on the site are tagged with code numbers and recorded with photographs, drawings, and often video cameras so that there is no question about where each artifact was located. In this way, it is very much like a traditional dig.

Some helmets allow divers to speak to each other as well as to those on the surface.

Divers use a watch to calculate their air supply.

Underwater excavations use plastic pipe to mark out squares and establish a solid grid.

Numbers indicate where the amphorae (storage jars) are located in the grid.

77

**Interesting Sites**

Over the years, some interesting underwater sites have been excavated. One was a freshwater well sacred to the Maya at Chichen Itza in Mexico. Chemicals were used to clear the silt and algae for better visibility, and divers were able to recover over 6,000 artifacts. Incense, copper, jade, and gold objects were found along with the bones of human sacrifices (many of whom were children).

The *Vasa* was a Swedish warship that sank in the harbor over 350 years ago. Divers dug tunnels under the bulk of the ship for the steel cables used to raise her. She is on display in a special museum in Stockholm today.

The *Vasa* was contained in a special support structure and sailed to shore through Stockholm's harbor, where it is now housed in a museum.

The *Mary Rose* was the flagship of King Henry VIII of England. It sank over 450 years ago. It took eleven years to excavate the wreck and raise the remaining half of her hull. Because the *Mary Rose* was quickly covered in silt, many artifacts were preserved. For example, no longbows had survived the centuries until many were discovered on the *Mary Rose*. Arrows were found as well. Both the long bows and arrows had to be excavated carefully since the wood had become the consistency of butter.

King Henry VIII's flagship, the *Mary Rose*, was excavated underwater with fabulous results.

78

One of the most celebrated ships of the twentieth century was the *Titanic*, which struck an iceberg and sank on her maiden voyage from England to America in 1912. The wreck was discovered in the mid 1980s, and has stirred up controversy ever since. The discoverer of the wreck believed it should remain untouched, yet others are bringing up objects (such as vases and china found strewn on the ocean floor) for display in museums. Should these items continue to be recovered, or should the ship be left intact as a monument where it rests on the ocean floor?

The *Titanic* remains in deep water on the bottom of the Atlantic Ocean, where it was discovered in 1985.

# Activity

### Research

Students research wrecks such as the *Vasa, Mary Rose, Titanic,* and others and present oral reports to the class.

### Panel Discussion

Students discuss pros and cons of issues such as:

- Should treasure hunters excavate ships like the *Muestra Señora de Atocha* solely for the millions of dollars of gold, silver, and precious stones on board the wreck? Very little archaeological work was done. Who loses? Who wins?

- Should the *Titanic* be excavated, or should it be left as a monument to those who died when it sank?

79

# Dating and Conserving Artifacts

> ### *Vocabulary:*
>
> **Carbon-14** or **radiocarbon dating**—technique used to detect how much radioactive carbon (or C-14) is in an organic artifact in order to tell how long ago it died
>
> **chronology**—arranging events in the order in which they occurred
>
> **context**—the place or situation from which things come and how they relate to one another
>
> **decay**—to decompose or diminish
>
> **in situ**—Latin phrase meaning "in place;" excavated artifacts are recorded in situ before removing them from the field
>
> **pothunters**—derogatory term to describe grave robbers and others who disturb ancient sites to retrieve artifacts they can sell for profit
>
> **radioactive**—having atoms that decay and send out radiation
>
> **thermoluminescence (TL)**—technique used to date pottery by measuring the amount of light produced when a sample is heated to very high temperatures
>
> **topology**—knowing typical artifacts from specific time periods.

## Chapter 15

### Context, Scientific Procedures, and the Evolution of Objects

The *context* of artifacts is the most important aspect of archaeology. In fact, all of the meticulous record-keeping procedures are meant to properly record everything about the context of the artifacts—their location in relation to other artifacts and features and the strata in which they were found. Only by relying on the context can artifacts be properly dated and understood.

Artifacts alone—without context—tell us only from what materials the objects are made and their possible use. Animal bones have little meaning other than the type of animal to which they belonged. Human skeletons without context reveal only information about that individual and cannot be related to any culture, place, or time. Buildings by themselves show only how they were constructed. But if all these things are pieced together, an unlimited amount of information becomes available.

### Burial Sites

In burial sites, context is everything. Not until the artifacts are found buried with an individual do archaeologists know that the artifacts had special significance in the culture.

*Archaeology*
Copyright ©1999 by Incentive Publications, Inc., Nashville, TN.

Preserved burials contain objects deliberately placed with the deceased. These objects had meaning to the people who performed the burial. As a result, very detailed conclusions about ancient people and their societies can be drawn from them.

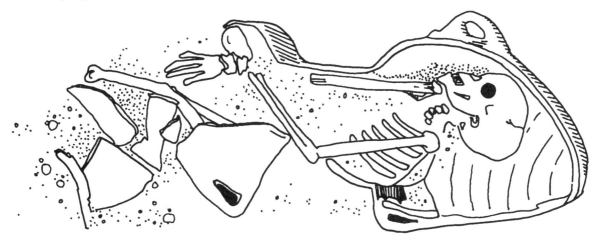

Skeleton in jar illustrates context

### In Situ

When archaeologists are excavating a site, they record all artifacts exactly as they found them, *in situ*—in place. Measurements are made, photographs are taken, sketches are made, maps are created, and field notes are taken before the artifacts are removed and catalogued.

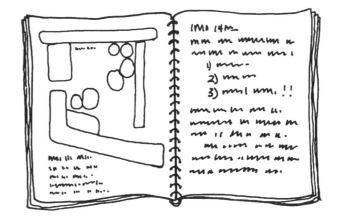

### Patterns of Activity

By noting where and what types of artifacts are found at a site, archaeologists can identify where human activity took place. For example, a religious area would have different artifacts than a cooking area. Discarded and useless animal bones can denote where animals were butchered, whereas larger meat-bearing bones can constitute an eating area.

Settlement and burial sites require that everything be in context before a detailed analysis can take place. This is why archaeologists are so enraged by *pothunters* who loot sites for valuable artifacts to sell. Even if an archaeologist later excavates the looted site, there is no way to interpret the findings since so much has been destroyed—stratigraphy, artifacts, and context.

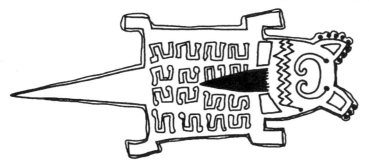

Without context, this gold ornament/artifact says nothing about when or by whom it was made.

81

## Coins

Coins are very useful for dating sites and interpreting different layers of stratification. Coins usually are minted with a date or identifiable ruler on them. If several coins are found buried at a site it can be dated to the date on the newest coin.

Coins are an excellent way to date a site.

## Dating Artifacts Using Scientific Procedures

Several scientific procedures have been developed to date archaeological finds. Until 1949 when Carbon-14 or *radiocarbon dating* was invented, the only way archaeologists could date anything was by combining stratigraphy (a sequence of layers) with *topology* (knowing typical artifacts from specific time periods). These methods, along with any historical records from a period, provided only a loose chronology until the dating of radioactive material became available.

Carbon-14 or radiocarbon dating created a revolution in archaeological dating. For the first time, dates could be determined using the artifacts themselves without concern for their context.

Carbon-14 dating works on organic (once living) material. Scientists know that a tiny amount of carbon in our atmosphere is radioactive. When a living thing dies, it stops taking in carbon 14 and the tiny amount of carbon 14 in it *decays* at a known rate. By measuring how much carbon 14 is in organic material such as bone, shell, or wood, scientists can determine how old it is.

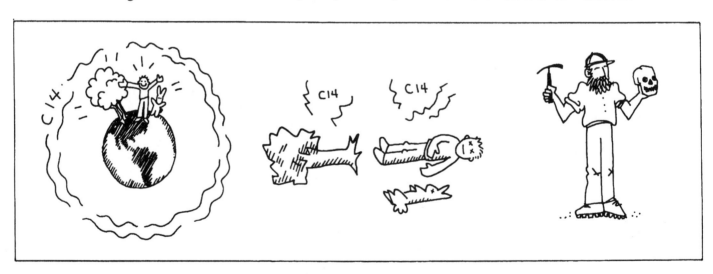

CARBON 14 (C14) EXISTS IN THE ATMOSPHERE, AND IT'S RADIOACTIVE. PLANTS AND ANIMALS NATURALLY TAKE IN SMALL QUANTITIES OF IT, SO C14 LEVELS IN LIVING ORGANISMS REMAIN CONSTANT DURING THEIR LIVES.

AFTER PLANTS AND ANIMALS DIE THE C14 LEVELS BREAK DOWN AT A KNOWN RATE (6,000 YEAR HALF LIFE).

WHEN ARCHAEOLOGISTS FIND PLANT OR ANIMAL REMAINS, THEY CAN TELL HOW OLD THE REMAINS ARE BY HOW MUCH C14 IS LEFT IN THEM.

*Thermoluminescence* (TL) is the scientific procedure used to date pottery. Since pottery is the most common artifact found at archaeological sites, this kind of dating not only determines the date of artifacts, but it can also detect forgeries.

Thermoluminescence requires heating the pottery sample to very high temperatures, then measures the minute amount of *radioactive* elements given off as light. The older the artifacts, the more light they create.

When pottery is fired, all trapped energy is released, setting the time clock at zero.

Over time, energy in the pot builds up, so . . .

When archaeologists expose the pot sample at high temperatures, it releases the stored energy as light. Measuring this light dates the pot.

Dendrochronology dates wood remains by counting tree rings and matching their growth pattern to known dates. Because the Carbon-14 in the atmosphere fluctuates, Carbon-14 dating (especially on objects dating from before 1000 B.C.) produced faulty dates that were more recent than they should have been. The use of dendrochronology helped solve this problem by using a tree-ring chronology dating back to 7500 B.C. When Carbon-14 dating of the wood is compared with the date determined by dendrochronology, a chart was produced that converted Carbon-14 dates to actual calendar dates. What resulted was a far superior method of archaeological dating.

The space between tree rings represents one year's growth. Cells carrying water are what tree rings are made of.

**Evolution of Objects**

Another way to date objects is to note how they have evolved over time. Shoes, for example, have served the same purpose for thousands of years, but their styles and the materials used to make them have change dramatically.

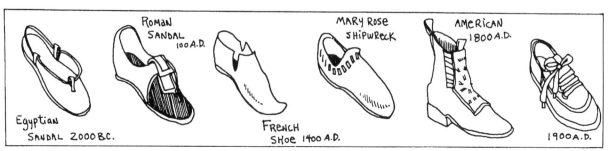

83

*Archaeology*
Copyright ©1999 by Incentive Publications, Inc., Nashville, TN.

# Activity: Ancient and Modern

### Materials
- Student Page 135

### Discussion

Discuss how everyday objects we take for granted—such as cars, bicycles, telephones, clothing and hair styles, modes of transportation, writing implements, sources of light, and so forth—have changed over the years.

1. *Need can opener to open*
2. *Pull tab detaches and opens top*
3. *Pop top opens can but does not detach.*

### Student Page 135

Students think about the ancient and modern items that serve the same purpose. This gives a good example of how objects have evolved over time.

### Research and Report

In pairs, students research one object that has evolved over time and present a report about it. Encourage students to bring in pictures, models, and actual articles to illustrate their findings.

# Activity: Scientific Methods of Dating Artifacts

### Materials
- artifacts from one of the previous activities in this book

### Discussion

Discuss the kind of dating to apply to specific artifacts, such as vases, carvings, bone spear points, and so forth.

Students decide which artifacts to date and which of the dating procedures to use. Note that not all artifacts need to be dated. Only representative samples are used to establish a chronology.

### Research

Encourage students to research other means of radioactive dating, how they work, and what they are used on:
- Potassium/Argon Dating (K/Ar)
- Fission Track Dating
- Magnetic Dating (dates changes in the Earth's magnetic polarity)

*Archaeology*
Copyright ©1999 by Incentive Publications, Inc., Nashville, TN.

# Activity: Context

## Mystery Artifact

### Materials
- unusual artifact students bring from home

Encourage students to bring odd and unusual artifacts from home. In small groups or whole group, discuss what can be known about the artifact without knowing its context. (List responses on board.) Then, have student reveal the context of the artifact and add what else can be learned from it to the list already on the board.

*My grandmother made this quilt when my mother and father got married. Mom said she will give it to me when I get married.*

Double Wedding Ring Quilt

This quilt is nothing but a blanket unless its story—its history—is known.

## Family Photos

### Materials
- old family photographs from students

After studying old photographs, students list what they can learn from a photo alone. Then, students put that information together with the context of the picture to gain greater knowledge.

*This photograph is of my grandfather and his family.*

Note how artifacts from students' own lives need context to be fully understood. Even old family photos loose meaning when no one in the picture can be identified. Without context, there is no meaning.

# Dating and Conserving Artifacts

---

**Vocabulary:**

**conservators**—people who conserve and preserve artifacts by processing or repairing them

**conserve**—to stabilize and preserve ancient objects so that no further decay occurs

**freeze-dry**—a way of preserving an object in which the object is frozen, then placed in a vacuum where ice is removed in the form of gas

**joins**—places where potsherds fit together

**polyethylene glycol (PEG)**—a liquid wax that slowly replaces water and hardens; often used to conserve wooden and leather artifacts

**preserve**—to keep an item intact so that it won't decay

**reconstruct**—to put pieces back together to form the whole artifact

**restore**—to attempt to make an artifact appear as it did originally

---

## Chapter 16

### Conserving Artifacts

Once excavated, an artifact is removed from the environment that preserved it. In fact, when archaeologists opened a 10,000-year-old tomb in Jericho, all the wooden furniture began crumbling before their eyes because of exposure to air. To stop the decay, they had to coat the furniture with wax to seal it from further exposure.

Usually an artifact survives because it was encased in an oxygen-free environment. Since the bacteria that cause decay need oxygen to live, the artifact was not subjected to destructive forces. Once it is exposed to the air, the process of decay begins immediately. So, archaeologists have a two-fold job—one is to carefully excavate and record each artifact and step of their progress; the other is to *preserve* the artifact for future study.

Whether artifacts are made of wood, metal, or pottery, there are special ways to *conserve* and preserve them for future study and enjoyment.

*Archaeology*
Copyright ©1999 by Incentive Publications, Inc., Nashville, TN.

## Wood and Leather

Wooden or leather objects that have been preserved in water (usually underwater or in a bog) must not dry out because they have weakened over time. They are often kept in tanks of water where *Polyethylene Glycol* (PEG) is added to force the water out and replace it with liquid wax, which hardens and strengthens the artifact.

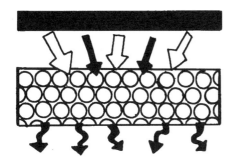

Polyethylene Glycol (PEG) is a liquid wax used to slowly replace the water in waterlogged wood and leather. As it hardens, it strengthens and preserves the object. The wooden hull of the Vasa is being impregnated with PEG.

Another way to preserve these artifacts is to *freeze-dry* them. This process is faster than PEG. First, the object is frozen. Then, it is placed in a vacuum chamber where the ice is transformed into gas and drawn off in a matter of weeks.

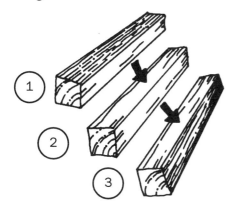

1. Wet artifact is frozen.

2. Ice is drawn from artifact as a gas in a vacuum chamber.

3. The final artifact is preserved as freeze-dried.

Many of the Mary Rose's wooden artifacts were preserved by freeze-drying.

## Metal

Metal objects usually have undergone some decay before being excavated. This is because most metals react with oxygen to form metal oxides that break down the metal. Iron objects, for example combine with oxygen to form iron oxide (or rust), which can completely destroy iron artifacts.

87

Sometimes x-rays help *conservators* "see" inside a corroded metal artifact to determine if there are elaborate designs underneath. If so, the artifact might be processed differently to avoid spoiling the design.

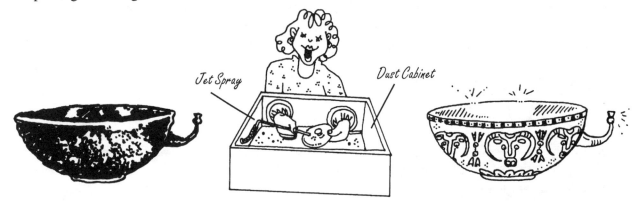

Corroded bowl

The bowl is cleaned with a jet spray of particles. The particles are then sucked out in a sealed cabinet.

The finished bowl is protected with polyester resin.

Other metal objects can be treated in a chemical bath to remove corrosion or, as in the case of the guns from the Mary Rose, heated in a special oven.

This is a controversial way of preserving ancient iron: heating it in a hydrogen atmosphere where the rust is converted back to metallic iron. The guns of the Mary Rose were conserved this way. Some experts think this is bad for the metal.

**Pottery**

Because pottery sherds are the most common artifacts, not all pieces are kept, and only special pots are reconstructed. First, all the pieces are washed and the *joins* are found and marked with chalk. Once all the joins are found, the pot is laid out on a flat surface with all pieces placed in proper position. Then the gluing begins.

Pottery sherds in pieces

Gluing pieces

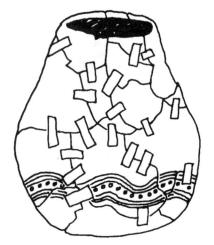

Glued pot with tape

*Archaeology*
Copyright ©1999 by Incentive Publications, Inc., Nashville, TN.

## The Iceman

Significant frozen finds, such as those of the Iceman and the Siberian frozen tombs, must be kept frozen to prevent rapid deterioration. In the case of the Iceman, his remains are kept in a freezer at a constant temperature. His body is removed for study for only 20 minutes at a time, then returned to the freezer. At most, he can be taken from the freezer only twice a day.

When archaeologists handle the Iceman, or any other delicate artifacts, they wear surgical gloves to prevent the oils on their hands from causing further deterioration.

Iceman is kept in a freezer at a constant temperature. He is taken out for only 20 minutes at a time and no more than twice a day.

## Paintings

Conserving or restoring paintings takes many forms. On Crete, only fragments of frescoes remain from Minoan times, but small scenes have been restored using these fragments as a guide. The cave paintings of Lascaux in France were deteriorating so badly because of the humidity and bacteria brought in by so many tourists that a second cave was painted to resemble the original. It is the second cave tourists see now, not the original.

Tomb paintings in Egypt have also been affected by tourists, so some tombs have been closed to tours.

Leonardo da Vinci's famous Sistine Chapel paintings were also affected by centuries of exposure to light and humidity. Over a period of several years, the paintings were painstakingly cleaned and restored by an international team of specialists. A climate-controlled system has been installed in the chapel where variables of light and humidity are carefully monitored to preserve the paintings for centuries to come.

Once conserved, artifacts are stored for study by archaeologists or displayed at museums for the public to enjoy.

89

# Activity: Reconstructing a Pot

### Materials
- Student Page 136
- terra-cotta pots (one per each pair of students)
- colored marking pens (permanent are best)
- large, plastic, resealable bags (one per each pair of students)
- masking tape
- white glue
- sand
- chalk
- plastic bowls

### Discussion
Discuss paintings and other pictorial ways ancient cultures have left information for archaeologists to interpret.

## Student Activity

In pairs, students imagine a civilization. It can be an actual civilization or one they make up themselves. They then draw pictures about their culture around a terra-cotta pot. Once done, they drop and break the pot, then place the pieces in their plastic bag.

Once potsherds are in plastic bags, proceed to Student Page 139.

### Student Page 136
Students follow directions to reconstruct a pot and interpret the civilization from the illustrations.

## Extensions

### Acropolis
Learn about conservation efforts to save the Parthenon on Athens' Acropolis.

### Abu Simbel
Research the international project of preserving Egypt's monument Abu Simbel when the Aswan dam was built.

### Sistine Chapel
Report on the detailed restoration of Leonardo da Vinci's famous paintings on the Sistine Chapel in Rome. Learn about the controversy raised by some experts.

# Famous Archaeologists, Sites, and Finds

---

**Vocabulary:**
**aerial**—view from the air or aircraft
**antiquities**—objects dating to ancient times
**benefactor**—person who gives financial help for a project
**earthwork**—an artificial mound or structure made of earth
**hewn**—shaped with cutting tools
**megalith**—huge stone used in building prehistoric monuments
**plunder**—taking goods and money forcibly or systematically

---

## Chapter 17

## Famous Finds, Mysteries, and Questions

There have been many colorful characters in the ranks of archaeologists from the infancy of the science through modern times. There is a streak of Indiana Jones that runs through the veins of all of them. They certainly are adventurers to brave the heat, the cold, and foreign conditions to excavate their sites. Instead of glamour, however, weeks of back-breaking work are required to move tons of dirt and painstakingly piece together the story of the site using artifacts. Actually, after the artifacts are excavated, cleaned, and catalogued, it can take years before the full story of the site is told. Often, finds raise more questions than they answer. Other times, a single artifact can reveal the story of a site. Then, on rare occasions, there are spectacular finds that shed light on aspects of ancient life never known before.

**Early Archaeology**

Until the early 1800s there was little interest in a scientific search for artifacts. Antiquities were sought and *plundered* for their value. Often they were sold to museums or private collectors for large sums of money. Unfortunately, this practice continues today, but there are international laws now forbidding looting. If perpetrators are caught, they can serve time in jail and face heavy fines. Back in the 1800s, no such laws existed. So some of the earliest "archaeologists" were little more than treasure hunters and thieves.

# Famous Finds

One of the first scientific archaeological endeavors was attached to Napoleon's 1798–1800 army campaign into Egypt. Along with his military units, Napoleon included a group of scientists. They studied and recorded Egyptian monuments. They also discovered the Rosetta Stone, which was covered in Greek and hieroglyphics. This major discovery resulted in deciphering hieroglyphics that had previously eluded scholars. This sparked an interest in Egypt that culminated in Howard Carter's discovery of King Tutankhamen's tomb.

## Howard Carter and Tut's Tomb

Howard Carter was an archaeologist excavating in Egypt. He was employed by Britain's Lord Carnarvon, a private collector with an interest in Egyptian antiquities. Carter made several spectacular finds for his *benefactor*, but in 1921, Lord Carnarvon doubted if further expense was necessary after several successful seasons of excavating. Carter convinced him to finance one more season. Carnarvon agreed to do so.

In November of 1922, Carter discovered a staircase leading down to a sealed door of a royal tomb. Most Egyptian tombs had been robbed in antiquity, but this one seemed intact. Carter sent a message to Carnarvon, who quickly came to Egypt to be with Carter when the tomb was opened. What they saw continues to dazzle the world.

Howard Carter discovered the only royal Egyptian tomb found intact. This room was called the Treasury.

Literally hundreds of items were found in the tomb. It remains the only royal Egyptian tomb discovered intact.

## Dead Sea Scrolls

Another spectacular find occurred in the Middle East in 1948.

The story is told that a shepherd boy was climbing the cliffs above the ruins of Qumran in search of a stray sheep. He was throwing rocks into the caves that honeycomb the hills to flush out the sheep when he heard something shatter. Upon closer investigation, he discovered a broken pottery jar with a scroll inside. That scroll turned out to be the "Temple Scroll," the largest scroll of the Dead Sea Scrolls.

92

When many other caves were studied, thousands of fragments of ancient scrolls were found. They are still being carefully studied today because they shed light on our understanding of the Old Testament of the Bible.

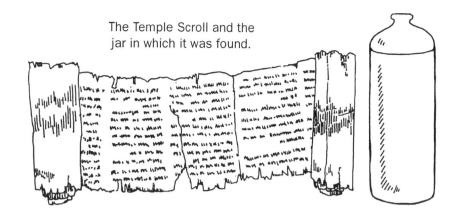
The Temple Scroll and the jar in which it was found.

## Xi'an Terra-Cotta Army

In China while digging a well, workers stumbled upon some life-sized terra-cotta soldiers. Later, archaeologists unearthed thousands of ceramic soldiers, horses, and chariots. They guarded the burial tomb of China's first emperor, Ch'in Shih Luang-ti.

## Mary Rose

Recovery of the Mary Rose, the flagship of King Henry VIII of England, presented scholars with a great deal of information on all aspects of shipbuilding, military armaments, and the conditions and outfitting of soldiers from that era.

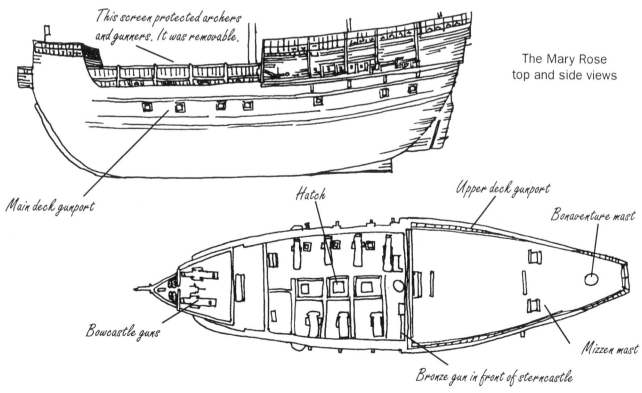
This screen protected archers and gunners. It was removable.

The Mary Rose top and side views

Main deck gunport

Bowcastle guns

Hatch

Upper deck gunport

Bonaventure mast

Mizzen mast

Bronze gun in front of sterncastle

93

### Ice Man

The recent discovery of a 5,000-year-old corpse in the Alps has shed light on life in prehistoric Europe.

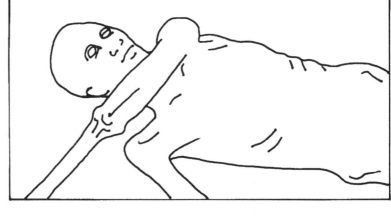

The Iceman,
as he was found

# Mysteries

Along with interesting discoveries come puzzling remains that only generate questions with few answers.

### Nazca Plains

High on a plateau in Peru are large images that can only be seen from the air. Spiders and many other shapes were worked into the plateau's soil for unknown reasons. There was no technology that allowed the Nazca people to view their work from our *aerial* perspective. And there is no evidence of extraterrestrial aid.

The Nazca Indians of Peru made huge images
on the ground that can be seen only from the air.
The reason they did this remains a mystery.

### Mound Builders, Megaliths, and Earthworks

In Britain and the United States there are the remains of prehistoric mounds built thousands of years ago. Some of the mounds house tombs for ancient chieftains or kings, while others appear to have been hill forts with trenches dug and walls mounded high for defense. Other mounds are clearly man-made, but their purpose has yet to be understood.

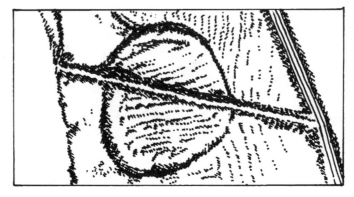

An Iron Age hill fort in eastern England

94

Britain's Stonehenge is a *megalithic* site that is not fully understood. Large hewn stones were brought great distances to be erected in a circular pattern. *Earthworks* were also part of the grand structure. Although scientists have determined that some of the stones were aligned with certain stars and other celestial bodies, the full significance of the site remains a mystery.

Stonehenge

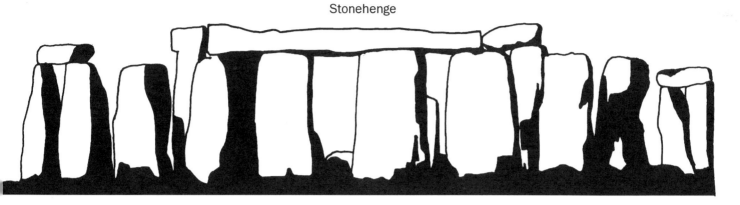

Native Americans also constructed large earthworks. The Adena people constructed the Serpent Mound along with other mounds in present-day Ohio. Serpent Mound appears to have been a religious monument and part of a structured landscape that once included villages and burials. The full significance may never be known since countless mounds have been looted of their artifacts.

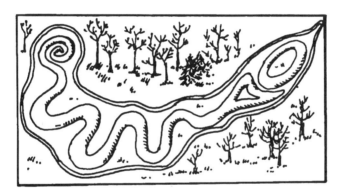

In Ohio, the Serpent Mound was built by the Adena people as a religious monument.

Such looting not only robs sites of their treasures, but it robs us all of their full significance. It cheats us of the story of our ancestors and the rich history that is part of our heritage.

# Dilemmas

These and other archaeological dilemmas continue to plague the scientists, scholars, and governments of the world.

### Elgin Marbles

In the early days of archaeology the great museums of the world paid people to bring back *antiquities* for display. This was done largely in the Eastern Mediterranean area before laws governing the wholesale looting of antiquities were enacted.

Grand monuments and exquisite sculptures and friezes were shipped back to these museums and put on display. One set of friezes came from the Parthenon in Athens, Greece. They are from the front and sides of the temple.

95

The Elgin Marbles were taken to the British Museum from the Parthenon in Athens, Greece.

Now known as the "Elgin Marbles," they are on permanent display at the British Museum in London. The dilemma these friezes represent is a common one . . . to whom do they belong? At first the question seems simple until further details come to light.

Athens is rapidly loosing its ancient monuments due to serious air pollution that results in acid rain. The marble, which is easily damaged by the acidic water, turns to soft limestone and slowly crumbles and disintegrates when exposed to these pollutants. The Parthenon is crumbling. If the Elgin Marbles had remained on the Parthenon, they would have crumbled beyond recognition and repair by now. But, by being housed in the British Museum, they have been preserved.

Greece says the marbles belong to them because it was their ancestors—the ancient Greeks—who made them. Britain says they have paid for the marbles by paying those who brought them to London.

To whom the marbles really belong remains a dilemma.

**Troy's Gold**

Another dilemma involves the gold objects found by Heinrich Schliemann when he excavated the remains of ancient Troy. He brought back gold funerary masks and other objects, including hundreds of gold beads, to a German museum. The objects remained in Germany until World War II.

When the city of Berlin was liberated from the Nazis in 1945, Troy's gold was missing along with other priceless treasures. Their whereabouts remained a mystery until the 1990s when a Russian museum found them crated in a storage room.

To whom does Troy's gold belong?

The Russians say it belongs to the world, but should remain in their possession because of the heavy losses their country suffered at the hands of the Germans during World War II. The Germans say it belongs to them because Heinrich Schliemann himself presented them to the museum. Turkey (the country in which ancient Troy is located) says the gold belongs to them since it was excavated there. To whom Troy's gold belongs remains a dilemma.

# Activity

### Research Archaeologists

Students research an archaeologist and report on him or her from a first-person perspective. They dress up and tell of their experiences.

### Archaeologists can include:
Kathleen Kenyon
Yigel Yadin
William Flinders Petrie
Heinrich Schliemann
Howard Carter
Giovanni Belzoni
Sir Leonard Wooley
Hiram Bingham

### Research Famous Sites

Students research famous archaeological sites and construct models of them. They then may write a description of the site or explain it to the class.

### Famous sites include:
Pompeii
Herculaneum
Troy
Mesa Verde
Machu Picchu
Stonehenge
Ankor Wat
Xi'an Terra-Cotta Army
Teotihuacan
King Tut's tomb
Masada
Great Zimbabwe
Pyramids of Egypt
Chichen Itza
Lascaux Cave
Ephesus
Iceman
Mary Rose

### Panel Discussions on Dilemmas

In small groups, students research the Elgin Marbles or Troy's gold dilemmas. They then hold panel discussions with two groups, each arguing a side of the dilemma.

97

# Experimental Archaeology

**Vocabulary:**

**adaptation**—something that is changed or changes for a new use or situation

**apothecary**—a druggist or pharmacist

**experimental archaeology**—hands-on approach to archaeology where ancient tools and techniques are replicated

**layperson**—someone who does not have specialized training in a particular subject

**Neolithic** (neo = new, lithic = stone)—new Stone Age; when stone tools were finely made, polished, and specialized

**replicate**—to repeat, duplicate, or construct a copy of

## Chapter 18

## Hands-On Approach to Archaeology

Recently, archaeologists have gone a step further in their interpretation of sites and artifacts. They have constructed working farms and communities using the same architecture, building materials, tools, and other artifacts found when excavating. This hands-on approach is called *experimental archaeology*. It includes everything from making arrow heads from volcanic glass to replicating ancient farming techniques.

*Neolithic* farms and other historical communities have been reconstructed as living museums. They are working examples of how our ancestors lived and offer great insight into the past for archaeologists and *laypeople* alike.

### Neolithic Communities

Neolithic farms and lake communities have been built to test long-standing theories arising from countless Neolithic excavations. On the farms, not only are the tools and buildings *replicated*, but the crops planted and animals used are historically correct as well. In this way, ancient grains can be tested for their yield and resistance to disease. Ancient animal breeds are also studied for their unique *adaptations* and other qualities.

This breed of cattle is a descendant of an ancient breed of cattle that is now extinct. The cattle are pulling a replica of an ancient plow.

98

With the discovery of the 5,000-year-old Iceman and his Neolithic tools, archaeologists were able to add to their working knowledge of the community he may have come from. They believe it may be similar to the Neolithic lake community excavated and recreated in Europe. By analyzing the contents of the Iceman's stomach and the clothing he wore, the ancient food and clothing of his time have been replicated as well.

This artist's rendition of the Iceman reflects the artifacts and bits of material found with him.

## Historical Sites

Ancient sites are not the only ones worth duplicating. Important sites only a few hundred years old are also historically significant. In America, Native American sites have been replicated along with sites such as Plymouth Plantation and Colonial Williamsburg. Plymouth Plantation is built on the excavated remains of Plymouth Colony where the Pilgrims first came to the New World. It is a working plantation of the 1600s. Not only have the homes, gardens, and furniture been recreated, the life of each colonist has been painstakingly researched and is played by an actor/worker on the site. Each colonist speaks in the dialect of his or her region and tells of the life and the beliefs that led him or her to board the Mayflower and sail to America.

This replica of a Powhatan Indian house in Virginia was built with the same tools and materials used in the 1700s.

The original site of Plymouth Plantation has been rebuilt to resemble the original. It remains a working colony and a great example of experimental archaeology.

Colonial Williamsburg is another example of experimental archaeology at work. The homes of the 1700s colonial town have been restored, and all of the craftsmen and tradespeople work at their trades with vintage tools and techniques. These include wigmakers, carpenters, gunsmiths, and an *apothecary*.

Those who visit an experimental archaeological site or create one of their own gain a depth of understanding far greater than a summation of artifacts can provide.

99

# Activity: Eat an Ancient Meal

**Materials**
- Student Page 137
- food and utensils as listed on Student Page

By deciphering ancient documents and analyzing food remains and pictures depicted in art-work, archaeologists have a good idea what the ancients ate.

## Aztecs

The Aztecs introduced many new foods and crops to the Spanish. These include corn, toma-toes, potatoes, peanuts, pineapples, turkey, and avocados. It is difficult to think of Italian cook-ing without tomatoes, but until they were brought back from the New World, Europe did not know about them.

Similarly, the Aztecs had no dairy products in their diet until the Spanish introduced sheep, goats, and cattle to them.

The most enduring legacy the Aztecs gave the world, however, was chocolate!

## Egyptians

The ancient Egyptians grew many crops in the fertile mud the floodwaters of the Nile left behind each year. They enjoyed a wide variety of fruits and vegetables, such as figs, dates, mel-ons, pomegranates, and olives. Though they had fish and fowl in abundance, the mainstay of their diet was whole grain bread, green onions, cheese, and a beer made from fermented bread.

The Egyptians loved sweets and made many delicacies with honey.

## Greeks

The Greeks also enjoyed a wide variety of meat, dairy products, fruits, and vegetables. Most dishes included olive oil and garlic for flavoring. Yogurt, cheese, figs, pears, apples, grapes, let-tuce, and bread were all enjoyed at the dinner parties called symposium where men ate together without women.

Spring and summer were when the fruits of the land were at their most diverse. In winter, how-ever, there was little fresh food available, so preserved foods were eaten, including dried fruits and vegetables and meat that was pickled, smoked, or salted.

## Romans

Much like the Egyptians and Greeks, the Romans had a wide variety of food available to them. Favorites included nuts, mushrooms, artichokes, radishes, and eggs as well as bread, meat, cheeses and other fruits and vegetables. Family life was highly valued by the Romans, so eat-ing dinner included the entire family. Wealthy families had dining rooms in their villas that were called tricliniums which meant "three-couch room." There, couches were placed on three sides around a central table from which the family ate while lounging on the couches.

In large cities, the common people didn't have kitchens in their homes, so they ate out in tav-erns or picked up something like meat pies, pastries, salads, cheeses, fruits, vegetables, or nuts on the way to and from work—much like people do today!

*Archaeology*
Copyright ©1999 by Incentive Publications, Inc., Nashville, TN.

In small groups, students read about and then prepare an ancient meal using the information provided.

Students lounge around a triclinium and enjoy a feast of foods from many ancient cultures.

## Activity: Dress Like a Greek, Roman, or Egyptian

### Materials

• Student Page 138    • fabric and other items as needed

Using tomb paintings, sculptures, and scenes depicted on pottery, ancient clothing styles can be understood.

### Student Page 138

Students follow directions and dress like a Greek, Roman, or Egyptian.

A. A semicircle of cloth.

B. Notice the short tunic the men wore.

Toga worn over a tunic (Roman)

101

# Activity: Time Capsules

### Materials
- Student Pages 139 and 140
- materials as listed on Student Pages

### Discussion

Discuss the kinds of artifacts students can put in time capsules to reflect their individual life and times. Discuss artifacts their parents or grandparents would put in capsules to reflect their own life and time when they were the students' ages.

### Student Pages 139 and 140

Students follow directions to construct time capsules for themselves and their parents and/or grandparents.

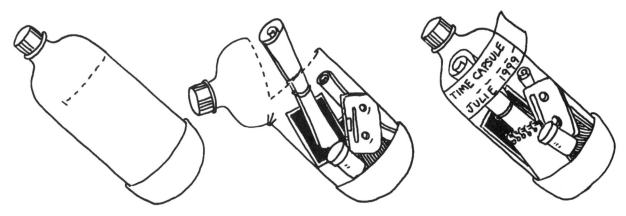

*NOTE: It is best not to bury the time capsule since moisture can damage the contents. Instead, place it in the back of a closet or in a box of family treasures for future discovery.*

# Activity: Mosaics, Frescoes, and More

Individually or in small groups, students construct a mosaic, fresco, or other piece of ancient art.

Pompeii mosaic

Minoan fresco

102

# Activity: Models

Students construct models of ancient tombs, buildings, or artifacts. They then write a brief description of it and explain it to the class.

This life-sized boat was buried near the pyramids
to carry the pharaoh into the next life.

Mayan stele shows ballplayers dressed in elaborate costumes.

# Activity: Create and Excavate a Site

**Materials**
- large cardboard boxes (one for each group)
- old sheet or plastic garbage bags to line each box
- sand or soil to fill each box
- trowels, brushes, and sieves
- artifacts

Students discuss what they have learned about archaeology and how to apply that to creating their own site (stratigraphy, dating artifacts, forensic information, and so forth). They then collect artifacts to reflect the kind of site they are creating, place them in their boxes, and fill the boxes with soil or sand.

103

### Excavating Site

Students exchange "sites" and excavate using tools and recording artifacts. Then they analyze the artifacts and present a "paper" at the Archaeological Conference that has been convened to share their results.

## Activity: Archaeological Conference and Museum

This is the culminating activity for the entire Archaeology Unit. Students display artifacts, models, and other projects in the class "museum," then present the results of their "digs" at the conference (which will amount to an oral report to the class). They may also wish to dress up as a noted archaeologist and tell about their important discovery.

104

# Archaeology Pre- and Post-Test

**True/False:** Circle T for True and F for False.

T  (F)  1. Archaeologists are digging primarily for gold artifacts.

T  (F)  2. Ancient historians' accounts are always true.

(T)  F  3. Archaeologists can learn about the past by studying ancient art.

T  (F)  4. An artifact is an ancient piece of art.

(T)  F  5. The difference between *prehistory* and *history* is the advent of writing.

(T)  F  6. Most of the items archaeologists find were lost or thrown away in antiquity.

(T)  F  7. The most common artifact is pottery.

T  (F)  8. All mummies come from Egypt.

**Specialists and Artifacts:** Draw and label the artifacts each specialist studies.

| 9. **Paleobotanist** | 10. **Paleographer** | 11. **Forensic Archaeologist** |
|---|---|---|
| pollen -ancient plant remains -fossilized pollen | Rosetta Stone -ancient writings & inscriptions | bones -human body remains mummy |

| 12. **Numismatist** | 13. **Ceramic Technologist** | 14. **Dendrochronologist** |
|---|---|---|
| Coin or medal - old coins (and often medals) | pieces of pottery & pots -determine construct, use, when, how, & where pottery was made | -dates wooden artifacts by analyzing tree ring growth wood |

**Categorization:** Circle the one that does not belong.

| 15. papyrus | 16. (mosque) | 17. Pompeii | 18. trowel | 19. survey |
|---|---|---|---|---|
| scroll | mosaic | Herculaneum | sieve | (amphora) |
| (quipu) | fresco | Mt. Vesuvius | (minaret) | feature |
| parchment | frieze | (Mary Rose) | brush | test trench |

105

## Matching: Draw a line from the word to its definition.

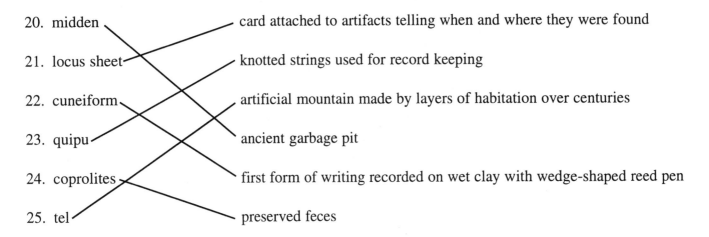

20. midden — card attached to artifacts telling when and where they were found

21. locus sheet — knotted strings used for record keeping

22. cuneiform — artificial mountain made by layers of habitation over centuries

23. quipu — ancient garbage pit

24. coprolites — first form of writing recorded on wet clay with wedge-shaped reed pen

25. tel — preserved feces

## Multiple Choice: Circle the correct answer.

26. The Rosetta Stone is important because . . .

    A. Napoleon found it.

    B. it was written in Greek.

    C. it helped decipher hieroglyphics. *(circled)*

    D. the British Museum needed a great artifact.

27. King Tutankhamen's tomb was important because . . .

    A. Heinrich Schliemann found it.

    B. it was the first royal Egyptian tomb found intact. *(circled)*

    C. little was known about mummies at the time.

    D. the mummy's curse was unleashed on the world.

28. In Situ means . . .

    A. Latin

    B. sit down

    C. on the ground

    D. in place *(circled)*

29. Which of these is _not_ a way to date artifacts?

    A. polyethylene glycol (PEG) *(circled)*

    B. context

    C. thermoluminescence (TL)

    D. radiocarbon dating

30. "Pothunting" is so destructive because . . .

    A. it ruins sites for future study.

    B. important artifacts are stolen.

    C. it is illegal.

    D. all of the above *(circled)*

## Written Responses

31. Give an example of conserving artifacts.

   *Possible answers include: (Reconstructing broken pots; freeze-drying some remains;*

   *frozen artifacts kept in freezers; impregnating wooden artifacts with PEG (polyethylene glycol);*

   *restoring corroded metal with chemical baths, by hand, or with special ovens.)*

32. Draw a stratified site. Explain it.

   *(In stratified sites, the deepest layer is the oldest. This is because the level of the ground rises over time due to people bringing in dirt on shoes and clothes. Wind, rain, floods, and other natural causes also raise ground levels.)*

33. Write what you know about one of these subjects:
   - Experimental Archaeology
   - Surveying an Area for a Site
   - Marine Archaeology
   - How Artifacts Are Preserved
   - Interpreting Ancient Art
   - Deciphering Ancient Writing

   **Subject:** _____

   *(Answers will vary depending on the subject.)*

## Post-Test Only

34. What was your most favorite part of the Archaeology unit? Explain why. *(Answers will vary.)*

35. What was your least favorite part? Why? *(Answers will vary depending on the subject.)*

36. What do you want to learn more about? Why? *(Answers will vary depending on the subject.)*

107

# Archaeology Pre- and Post-Test

**True/False:** Circle T for True and F for False.

T F 1. Archaeologists are digging primarily for gold artifacts.

T F 2. Ancient historians' accounts are always true.

T F 3. Archaeologists can learn about the past by studying ancient art.

T F 4. An artifact is an ancient piece of art.

T F 5. The difference between *prehistory* and *history* is the advent of writing.

T F 6. Most of the items archaeologists find were lost or thrown away in antiquity.

T F 7. The most common artifact is pottery.

T F 8. All mummies come from Egypt.

## Specialists and Artifacts: Draw and label the artifacts each specialist studies.

| 9. **Paleobotanist** | 10. **Paleographer** | 11. **Forensic Archaeologist** |
|---|---|---|
| 12. **Numismatist** | 13. **Ceramic Technologist** | 14. **Dendrochronologist** |

## Categorization: Circle the one that does not belong.

| 15. papyrus | 16. mosque | 17. Pompeii | 18. trowel | 19. survey |
|---|---|---|---|---|
| scroll | mosaic | Herculaneum | sieve | amphora |
| quipu | fresco | Mt. Vesuvius | minaret | feature |
| parchment | frieze | Mary Rose | brush | test trench |

Name _____

*Archaeology*
Copyright ©1999 by Incentive Publications, Inc., Nashville, TN.

## Matching: Draw a line from the word to its definition.

20. midden                card attached to artifacts telling when and where they were found

21. locus sheet           knotted strings used for record keeping

22. cuneiform             artificial mountain made by layers of habitation over centuries

23. quipu                 ancient garbage pit

24. coprolites            first form of writing recorded on wet clay with wedge-shaped reed pen

25. tel                   preserved feces

## Multiple Choice: Circle the correct answer.

26. The Rosetta Stone is important because . . .

   A. Napoleon found it.

   B. it was written in Greek.

   C. it helped decipher hieroglyphics.

   D. the British Museum needed a great artifact.

27. King Tutankhamen's tomb was important because . . .

   A. Heinrich Schliemann found it.

   B. it was the first royal Egyptian tomb found intact.

   C. little was known about mummies at the time.

   D. the mummy's curse was unleashed on the world.

28. In Situ means . . .

   A. Latin

   B. sit down

   C. on the ground

   D. in place

29. Which of these is _not_ a way to date artifacts?

   A. polyethylene glycol (PEG)

   B. context

   C. thermoluminescence (TL)

   D. radiocarbon dating

30. "Pothunting" is so destructive because . . .

   A. it ruins sites for future study.

   B. important artifacts are stolen.

   C. it is illegal.

   D. all of the above

Name _____

## Written Responses

31. Give an example of conserving artifacts.

_____

_____

_____

32. Draw a stratified site. Explain it.

_____

_____

_____

_____

_____

33. Write what you know about one of these subjects:
    - Experimental Archaeology
    - How Artifacts Are Preserved
    - Surveying an Area for a Site
    - Interpreting Ancient Art
    - Marine Archaeology
    - Deciphering Ancient Writing

    **Subject:** _____

    _____

    _____

    _____

    _____

## Post-Test Only

34. What was your most favorite part of the Archaeology unit? Explain why.

_____

_____

35. What was your least favorite part? Why?

_____

_____

36. What do you want to learn more about? Why?

_____

_____

Name _____

# Locus Sheets

Cut out the locus sheets. Fill them out completely, and keep them with your artifacts.

## Locus Sheet

**Site:** _____     **Locus:** _____

Draw and number artifacts below.

List artifacts on correctly numbered line.

1. _____
2. _____
3. _____
4. _____
5. _____
6. _____
7. _____
8. _____
9. _____
10. _____

Name:_____

## Locus Sheet

**Site:** _____     **Locus:** _____

Draw and number artifacts below.

List artifacts on correctly numbered line.

1. _____
2. _____
3. _____
4. _____
5. _____
6. _____
7. _____
8. _____
9. _____
10. _____

Name:_____

*NOTE: Run this on heavy paper or card stock for best results.*

# Who's Who

Draw and label your artifacts. Write questions each specialist would ask about them.

## Forensic Archaeologist:
studies human body remains

**Artifacts:** Draw and label below.

Questions: _____
_____
_____
_____

## Numismatist:
studies coins

**Artifacts:** Draw and label below.

Questions: _____
_____
_____
_____

## Paleobotanist:
studies plants and pollen

**Artifacts:** Draw and label below.

Questions: _____
_____
_____
_____

## Ceramic Technologist:
studies pottery

**Artifacts:** Draw and label below.

Questions: _____
_____
_____
_____

## Paleographer:
studies inscriptions and documents

**Artifacts:** Draw and label below.

Questions: _____
_____
_____
_____

## Dendrochronologist:
studies tree rings

**Artifacts:** Draw and label below.

Questions: _____
_____
_____
_____

Name _____

# Specialist Report

Draw and label artifacts, then analyze them. Write a report based on your findings.

**Archaeological Specialist:** _____

**Artifacts:** Draw and label below.

[ ]

**Report:** Write a report based on your conclusions about the artifacts above. Use additional paper as needed to complete your report.

_____

_____

_____

_____

_____

_____

Name _____

# Deciphering Ancient Writing

Below are examples of Egyptian hieroglyphics, Indus Valley glyphs and the Greek and Roman alphabets.
Practice using them to write your own messages.

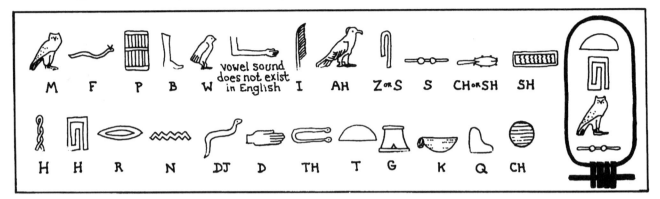

Egyptian hieroglyphics have signs standing for one or several letters of our alphabet.
Notice that only one vowel is present. The Egyptians primarily used consonants in their writing.

Indus Valley glyphs have yet to be deciphered.

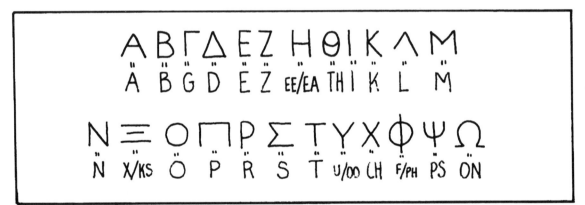

The Greek alphabet was adapted from the Phoenician. Many recognizable letters are used in it.

## A B C D E F G H I K L M N O P Q R S T V X Y Z

The Roman alphabet was adapted from the Greek. We recognize it as our alphabet, except for three missing letters.

Name _____

# Original Rosetta Stone

Create your own Rosetta Stone using English, hieroglyphics, and your own form of writing (try to include some Indus Valley glyphs in your own alphabet).

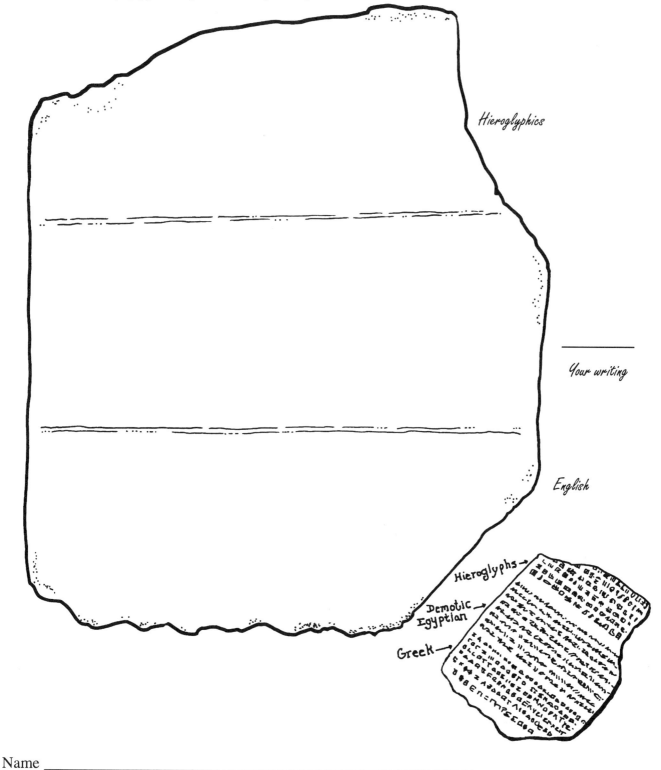

Name _____

# Make a Scroll and Be a Historian

Follow the directions to construct a scroll. Then be a historian. Give your account of a sporting event (as if it were a battle), an important world or local event, the seven wonders of your world, or detailed aspects of a day in your life.

**Materials:**
- 15 sheets of plain white paper (8½" x 11")
- 2 (12'–15') long handles (cut broom handles, long wooden spoons, or cardboard paper towel tubes work well)
- glue or double-stick tape

1. Glue or tape the 15 sheets of paper together to make a long scroll. (NOTE: Scrolls were made by gluing sheets of papyrus together or by stitching parchment together. They tended to be about 15 feet long.)

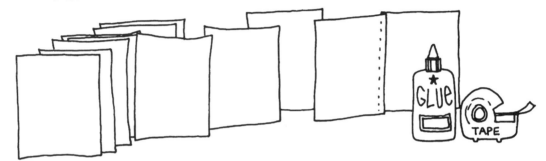

2. Attach the handles with glue or tape. (NOTE: Glue paper so that it completely surrounds handles to keep it from detaching.)

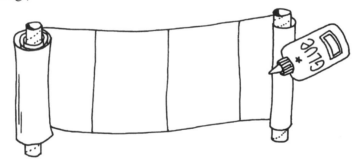

3. Write one column down each sheet of paper so that the scroll can be rolled and unrolled easily while reading.

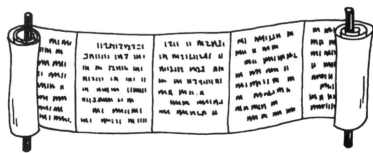

Name _____

*Archaeology*

## Interpreting Ancient Art

What can you tell about ancient life from these objects of art?

Greek vase with
olive harvest scene

Ivory carving of
a Viking warrior

Egyptian tomb painting of wheat harvest

Mosaic Map of ancient Jerusalem

Peruvian pot depicting a musician
with many instruments

Name _____

*Archaeology*
Copyright ©1999 by Incentive Publications, Inc., Nashville, TN.

# Research Art from a Significant Culture

Choose an ancient culture. Draw four pieces of art or artifacts from that culture. Then write what you can learn about the culture based on those pieces.

## Ancient Culture: _____

Draw and label four pieces of art or artifacts from this culture.

| | |
|---|---|
| | |

_____    _____

_____    _____

| | |
|---|---|
| | |

_____    _____

_____    _____

What conclusions about this culture can you draw from these artifacts? _____

_____

_____

_____

Name _____

# A Site Frozen in Time

Your favorite site is buried in a disaster. Draw a map of what archaeologists will find.

Student Name: _____

What kind of site is it? _____

How was it used? _____

Who used it? _____

What disaster buried it? _____

- - - - - - - - - - - - - - - - - - - - - - - - - - - - - - - - - -

Site Number_____

Draw a map of what would be found when this site is excavated. (Number and label objects below.)

Number the objects on the map above. Label them below.

1. _____     8. _____
2. _____     9. _____
3. _____    10. _____
4. _____    11. _____
5. _____    12. _____
6. _____    13. _____
7. _____    14. _____

Name _____

# Time Capsule Interpretation

Map the site created on Student Page 122 using the grid below. Label each artifact on the map. Then write an interpretation of what remained behind, what kind of site it was, how it was used, and who used it based on your information.

Archaeologist's Name: _____

What kind of site was it? _____

How did you reach that conclusion? _____

_____

_____

How was the site used?_____

What makes you think that? _____

_____

_____

Who used it? _____

How do you know? _____

Name _____

# Which Artifacts Tell Your Story?

Draw and list 10 artifacts that will tell about you in 100 years, as well as 10 artifacts that will tell about a parent or grandparent in 100 years.

| Me | Parent / Grandparent |
|---|---|
| | |

What might an archaeologist say about you based on your artifacts?_____

_____

_____

_____

What might an archaeologist say about your parents or grandparents based on their artifacts?

_____

_____

_____

Name _____

# My Stratified Life

Draw and label artifacts from your life at the appropriate level.

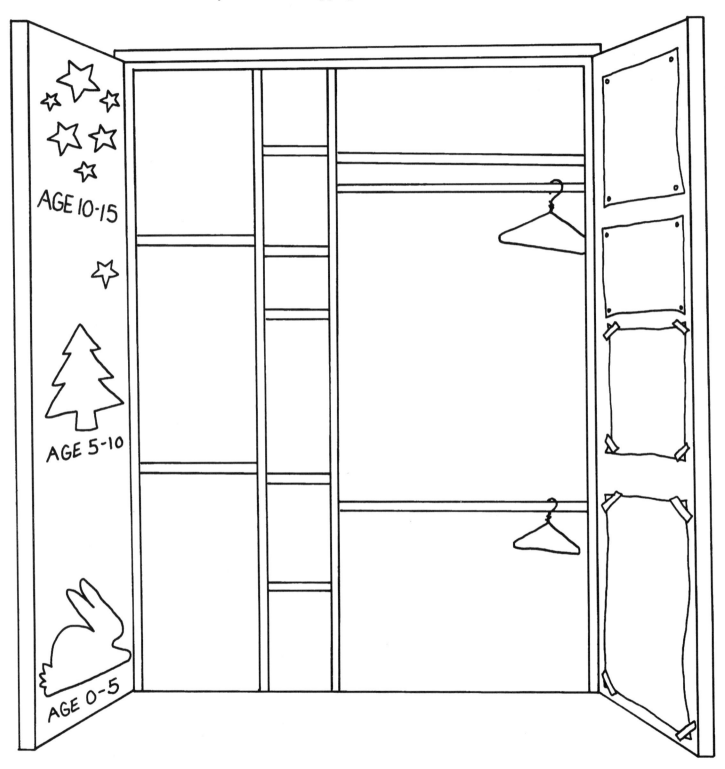

Name _____

*Archaeology*
Copyright ©1999 by Incentive Publications, Inc., Nashville, TN.

# How Artifacts Are Preserved

This experiment replicates the various conditions in which artifacts are found: dry, frozen, humid, under-water uncovered, and underwater covered.

Your group will need:
- 5 clear plastic cups
- 5 pieces of fruit
- plastic wrap
- pottery clay
- 1½ cups pea gravel
- masking tape and rubber bands

1.  Label cups with masking tape as follows:
    Dry, Humid, Frozen, Underwater Uncovered, Underwater Covered.

2.  Set up each cup according to these directions:

   **Dry:** Fill ⅓ of cup with gravel. Place fruit into the gravel so that it can still be seen. Place under a lamp to recreate the hot, dry conditions in which some artifacts are found.

   **Humid:** Fill ⅓ of cup with gravel. Place fruit on top of gravel. Add water until it just touches fruit. Cover with plastic wrap and seal with rubber bands. Store at room temperature.

   **Frozen:** Fill ⅓ of cup with gravel. Place fruit into gravel, then pour in more gravel until fruit is covered but can be seen through the cup. Fill cup with water and place in a freezer.

   **Underwater Uncovered:** Follow Frozen directions, but store in a refrigerator.

   **Underwater Covered:** Surround fruit with damp clay and press until it is airtight (do this with plastic wrap so that your hands won't get dirty). Fill 1/3 of cup with gravel and pour in water until it just begins to show on top of gravel. Place clay-covered fruit on gravel. Cover cup with plastic wrap and seal with rubber bands. Store in a refrigerator.

DRY            HUMID            FROZEN            UNDERWATER UNCOVERED            UNDERWATER COVERED

Check once a week and record results on the "Preserved Artifacts Observation" sheet.

Name _____

*Archaeology*
Copyright ©1999 by Incentive Publications, Inc., Nashville, TN.

# Preserved Artifacts Observation

Write your observations of each cup's artifact once a week for four weeks. Then record your conclusions about the conditions in which artifacts are best preserved.

| | Dry | Humid | Frozen | Underwater Uncovered | Underwater Covered |
|---|---|---|---|---|---|
| Week #1 | | | | | |
| Week #2 | | | | | |
| Week #3 | | | | | |
| Week #4 | | | | | |

Dry: _____

Humid: _____

Frozen: _____

Underwater Uncovered: _____

Underwater Covered: _____

Name _____

# Modern-Day Equivalent

Draw and label present-day items that would be stored in these ancient containers.

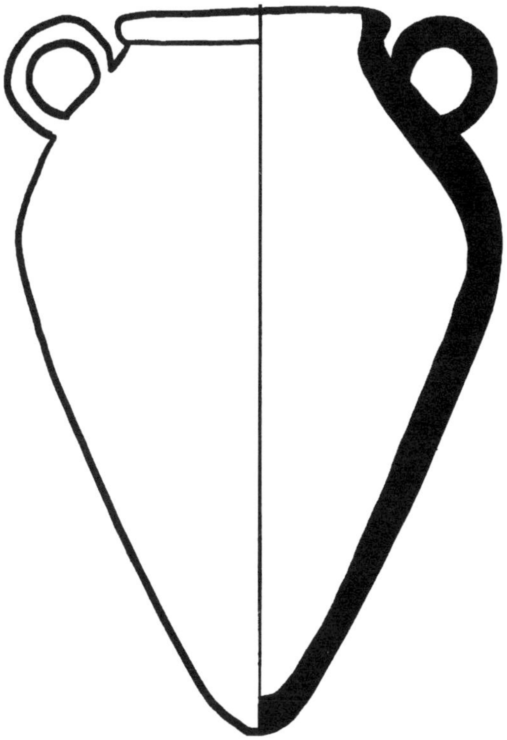

What would you store in this amphora?

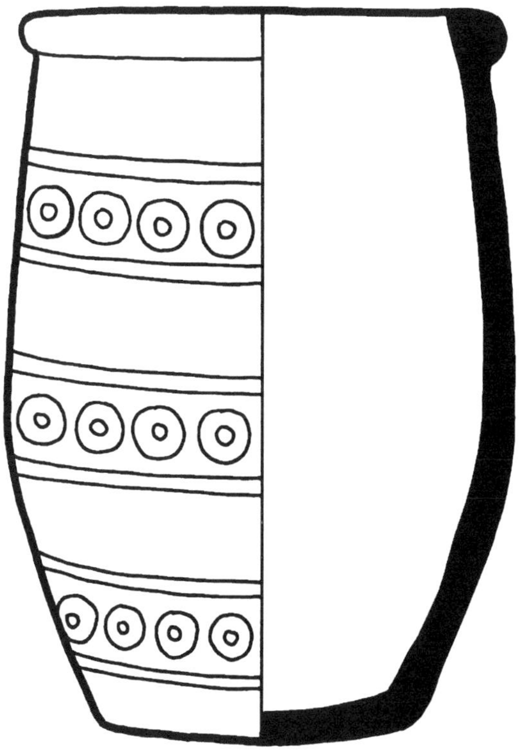

_____
_____
_____
_____
_____
_____
_____
_____

What would you store in this pithoi?

_____
_____
_____
_____
_____
_____
_____
_____
_____
_____

Name _____

# Pottery Diameter Scale

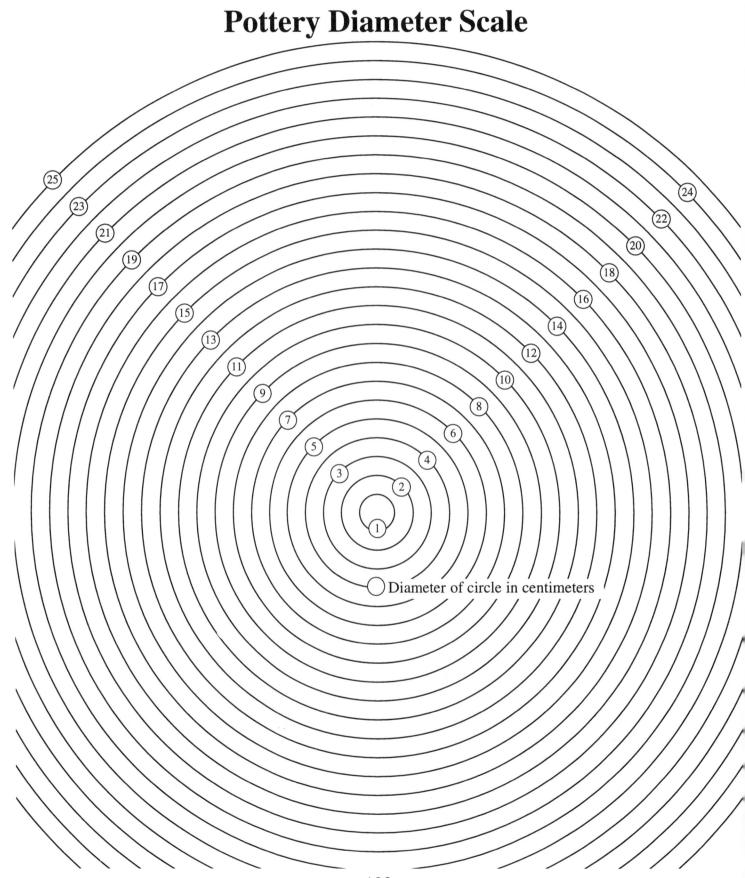

◯ Diameter of circle in centimeters

# **Pottery Diameter Scale**

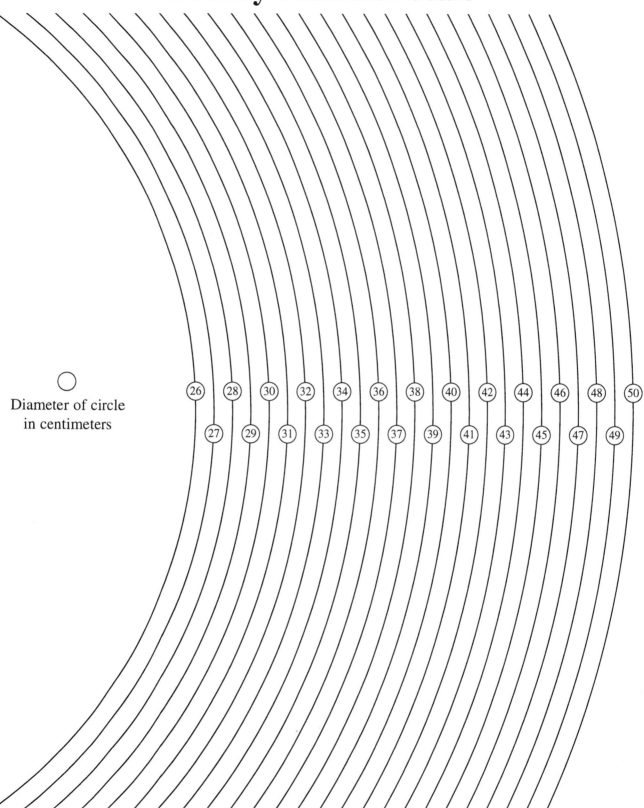

Diameter of circle
in centimeters

*Archaeology*
Copyright ©1999 by Incentive Publications, Inc., Nashville, TN.

# Schedule Comparisons

Below is the schedule of a dig in Jordan. Compare it with your everyday schedule.

**Dig Schedule in Jordan**                                        **My Schedule**

4:30 A.M.        Wake up                                          _____

5:00             1st breakfast
                 (hot cereal, fruit, pita bread)                  _____

5:30             Go to site, begin digging                       _____

7:30             Break (watermelon)(15 minutes)                   _____

9:00             2nd breakfast (30 minutes)
                 (falafel or schwarma, watermelon)                _____

10:30            Break (15 minutes)                               _____

12:30 P.M.       Return to camp and clean up                      _____

1:00             Lunch at camp for main meal
                 (baked chicken, sliced tomatoes and              _____
                 cucumbers, pita bread, humus, feta
                 cheese, watermelon)                              _____

2:00–4:00        Quiet time (rest)                                _____

4:00–6:00        Pottery washing; lab work
                 (cataloguing artifacts, numbering                _____
                 potsherds); specialists work on artifacts        _____

6:00             Dinner                                           _____

7:00–9:00        Class, lecture, or free time                     _____

9:00             Lights out                                       _____

Compare your day to a day on this dig.

_____

_____

_____

_____

*NOTE: You might try to follow this schedule for a day.*

Name _____

*Archaeology*
Copyright ©1999 by Incentive Publications, Inc., Nashville, TN.

# In Situ:

## *Newsletter for a Jordanian Tel Excavation*

*Editor: Judith Cochran*                                      *Vol. 2, No. 1*

### Welcome to the Adventure of a Lifetime

For those of you on your first dig, you've embarked upon the Adventure of a Lifetime in a country known for its generosity and hospitality. Enjoy it. Treasure it. Take photos, and write about it. No matter what your future holds, you can always look back on this experience and remember the people, the places, and all the little things that made it so special. The best advice is the simplest—protect yourself from sun and dust, stay rested and hydrated, and be open to new experiences. The rest will fall into place.

### What to Pack

Basics: 3 pairs long pants, 1 pair shorts, 2 short-sleeved shirts, 3 long-sleeved shirts, hat, gloves, 5–7 pairs underwear and socks, 2 pairs shoes, sweater, nice pants or skirt, toothbrush/toothpaste, comb, shampoo, laundry soap, pajamas, towel, sleeping bag, and pillow.
Extras: Other than the necessities, these small items can make your adventure more comfortable:
• small flashlight
• compact tape player
• insect repellent
• 8 to 10 favorite tapes
• lip balm and moisturizer
• travel clock
• favorite snacks (candy, gum)
• eye shades (to sleep if light is on)
• ear plugs (in case you are near a snorer)
• bandanna/respiratory mask (to keep from inhaling dust)
• prescriptions in original bottles
• other recommended medications: stomach relief medications, aspirin, sunscreen, eye drops, antiseptics for cuts
• $500 to $750 U.S. (add $250 for weekend tours)

### Proper Attire

When digging at sites, a hat, long pants, and sleeves are a must. Believe it or not, covered arms and legs are actually cooler than bare ones because clothes create a moist micro-climate to the skin that prevents dehydration. Within the confines of camp, shorts and T-shirts are acceptable. Outside the compound, however, it is recommended that men and women wear long pants and tops that are not revealing (preferably long-sleeved, especially for women). Also refrain from any public shows of affection. As guests in Jordan, dig members should be mindful of traditional Moslem standards of dress and decorum.

### Staying Hydrated

Water is serious business in the desert. You should consume 1½ to 2 liters of water a day. Caffeinated drinks (colas, coffee, tea) don't count toward the daily allowance since caffeine is a diuretic and furthers dehydration.
To insure you are hydrated: keep urinating; don't wait for thirst—drink water when your lips feel dry; wear long sleeves whenever in the sun.
If skin leaves an indentation when pressed, or ability to urinate stops, contact one of the directors.

### Jordan's Money and Communications Home

A dinar, or JD (for "Jordanian Dinar") is the money standard used in Jordan. One JD equals approximately $1.50 U.S. There are 1000 fils in each JD.
*Postage Rates to North America:*
  Postcard—250 fils, Letter—320 fils for 10 grams (about one page in an airmail envelope), 160 fils each additional 10 grams
*Fax:* 5–6 JD per page
*Phone Calls:* Phone access is limited, and calls are expensive.

### Turkish Toilets, Showers, and Electricity

Turkish toilets are akin to a sink in the floor with places to put your feet and squat. In Muslim countries, Turkish toilets are considered more sanitary because a toilet seat isn't used repeatedly.
Showers should be short since efficient water use is important in the desert. Hot water is available two hours a day, directly after returning from work at sites.
Dorms and bathrooms have no electrical outlets, making electric shavers, blow dryers, and curling irons useless. Self-contained butane curling irons have been used successfully, but the best advice is to get a low-maintenance hair style and let nature take its course.

### Useful Arabic Terms

Below are some Arabic terms you may find useful:

| | |
|---|---|
| Thank you = SHUK - ran | Hello = mar - HA - ba |
| You're welcome = af - WAN | Good-bye = maal - sal - AME |
| Please = min - FAD - lak (m) | Yes = NAAM |
| Please = min - FAD - lik (f) | No = LA |

### Pizza Hut

Along with Neolithic and Roman remains, this is Amman's most distinguished landmark (according to past dig participants).

# Sample List of Sites

Below is a sampling of archaeological sites around the world.

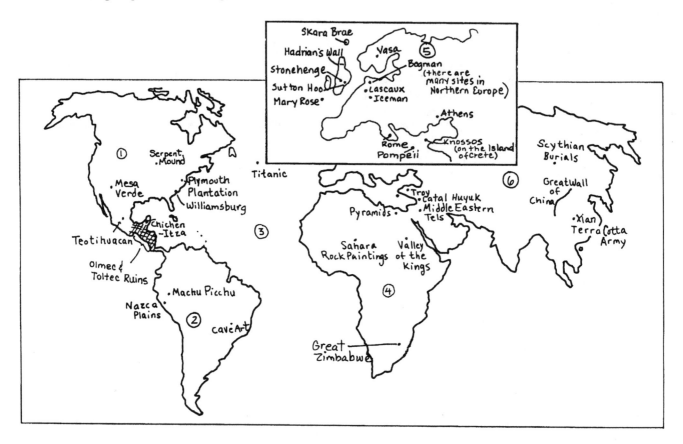

1. North America
   - Mesa Verde
   - Serpent Mound
   - Plymouth Plantation
   - Williamsburg
   - Olmec and Toltec Ruins
   - Chichen Itza
   - Teotihuacan

2. South America
   - Machu Picchu
   - Cave Art/petroglyphs
   - Nazca Plains

3. Atlantic Ocean
   - Titanic

4. Africa
   - Pyramids
   - Valley of the Kings/King Tut's Tomb
   - Sahara Rock Paintings
   - Great Zimbabwe

5. Europe
   - Hadrian's Wall
   - Stonehenge
   - Sutton Hoo
   - Skara Brae
   - Lascaux
   - Mary Rose
   - Pompeii/Herculaneum
   - Knossos
   - Athens
   - Iceman
   - Bogman
   - Vasa
   - Rome

6. Asia
   - Troy
   - Catal Huyuk
   - Scythian Burials (Siberia)
   - Xian Terra Cotta Army
   - Great Wall of China
   - Middle Eastern Tels

For more information about archaeological sites, contact: Archaeological Institute Of America, 135 William Street, New York, NY 10038; (212) 732-5154, FAX (212) 732-5707.

# Going on a Dig

# Where Would You Dig and Why?

Below are three sites with their features on a grid, which is divided into fields and squares. Decide which two squares in each site you would open first, and explain why.

Roman fort—Aerial photo of ground features

I would open squares _____ and _____

because _____

_____

_____

_____

_____

_____

Infrared photo site—Bronze Age burial circles

I would open squares _____ and _____

because _____

_____

_____

_____

_____

_____

GPR site—Casement walls at a Jordanian Tel

I would open squares _____ and _____

because _____

_____

_____

_____

_____

Name _____

131

# Going on a Dig

## Student Page

## Field Notes from a Tel in Jordan

Examine the balk drawings and map of the square. Write your interpretation of the site.

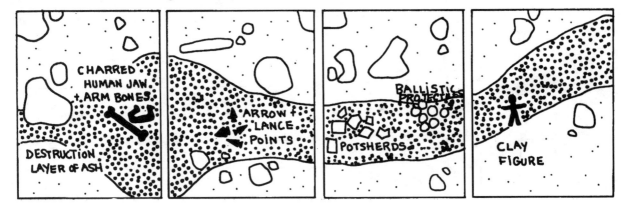

What is your interpretation of this square?

_____

_____

_____

_____

_____

_____

_____

_____

_____

_____

_____

What questions does this data raise? _____

_____

_____

_____

_____

_____

_____

_____

Name _____

132

*Archaeology*
Copyright ©1999 by Incentive Publications, Inc., Nashville, TN.

# Going on a Dig

# Stratigraphy Activity

Draw your stratified site to scale below.

Label, identify, and describe the material making up each strata below.
Example: Strata I = coarse blue pea gravel

**Strata** _____

**Strata** _____

**Strata** _____

**Strata** _____

**Strata** _____

Name _____

*Archaeology*
Copyright ©1999 by Incentive Publications, Inc., Nashville, TN.

# Explanation and Interpretation of a Stratified Site

Draw and label the artifacts in each layer. Then date each layer.

**Artifact and Description**

What is your explanation or interpretation of this site? _____

_____

_____

_____

_____

_____

_____

_____

_____

_____

_____

Name _____

*Archaeology*

# Ancient and Modern

Draw items used for the same purpose in ancient and modern times. Describe them.

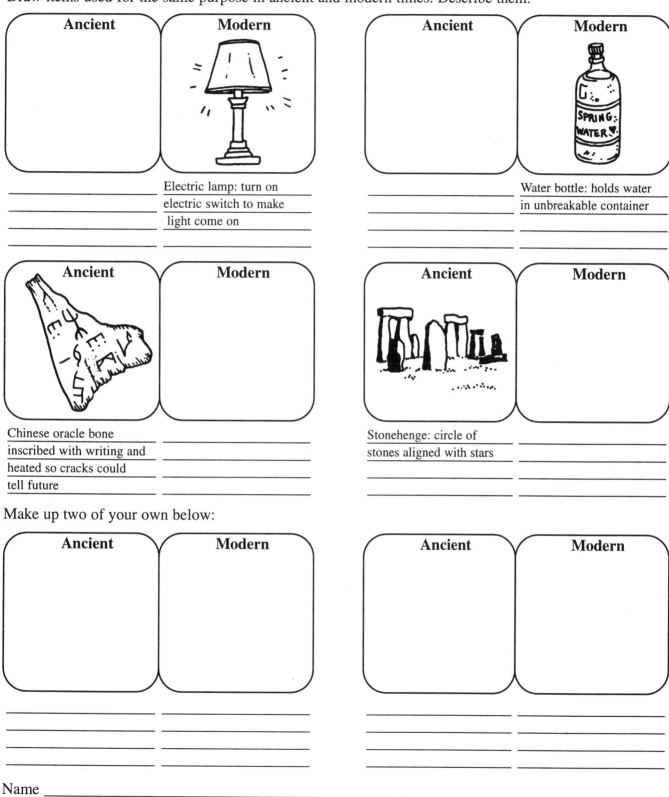

| Ancient | Modern |
|---|---|

Electric lamp: turn on
electric switch to make
light come on

| Ancient | Modern |
|---|---|

Water bottle: holds water
in unbreakable container

| Ancient | Modern |
|---|---|

Chinese oracle bone
inscribed with writing and
heated so cracks could
tell future

| Ancient | Modern |
|---|---|

Stonehenge: circle of
stones aligned with stars

Make up two of your own below:

| Ancient | Modern |
|---|---|

| Ancient | Modern |
|---|---|

Name _____

135

# Reconstructing a Pot

Follow these directions to conserve and reconstruct your pot.

**Materials:**     chalk           potsherds in plastic bag
                     white glue      sand in large plastic bowl
                     masking tape    fine felt-tipped marking pens

1. First, number all your potsherds with your identification number. For example: Jill and Andy both have an August birthday so they chose "JA8" as their number.

2. Lay out your pot and find the joins. Mark them with chalk.

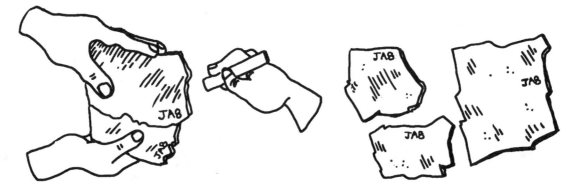

Joins are chalked.

3. Start at rim or base to reconstruct, depending on which is the most constructible. Spread a thin layer of glue on sherd and stick together. Stabilize with masking tape. Use sand to try to hold pieces at an angle to dry.

Standing the pieces in sand to maintain an angle may be necessary.
Tape is used to hold the joins in places while the glue hardens.

4. Study reconstructed pot illustrations and interpret them. Report your findings to the class.

Name _____

# Eat an Ancient Meal

Use the information below to prepare an ancient meal.

## AZTECS:

The favorite drink of the Aztecs was chocolate, or chocolatl, as they called it. It was made from grinding up cacao beans and boiling them with corn flour, then straining and whipping the mixture into a stiff froth. Since they didn't have sugar, the Aztecs sweetened their chocolate with honey. Montezuma drank his chocolatl out of a gold cup.

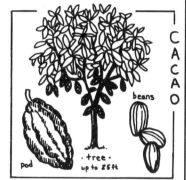

*Cacao beans were used as money in the Aztec Empire.*

### Aztec Chocolatl (serves 4)
You will need:

- 4 cups milk
- ½ tsp. ground cinnamon
- ½ lb. semisweet chocolate chips
- 2 drops vanilla
- honey to taste

1. Melt chocolate chips in microwave or over double boiler until smooth.
2. In another pan, heat milk (do not boil). Pour melted chocolate into milk; add cinnamon and vanilla. Bring to a boil.
3. Remove from heat and whisk mixture for two minutes until foamy.
4. Pour into mugs. Sweeten to taste with honey.

## EGYPTIANS:

Egyptians believed in cleanliness, but when it came to eating they ate with their fingers and rarely used utensils. Their servants brought scented water to the table and napkins so that everyone could wash their hands after a meal. Egyptians also enjoyed sweets. Bakers made bread and rolls sweetened with nuts and honey. Tiger Nut Sweets were very popular.

### Tiger Nut Sweets (serves 4)
You will need:

- 7 oz. dates
- 2–3 tbsp. water
- ¼ cup honey
- ¼ cup chopped walnuts
- ¼ cup ground almonds
- ½ tsp. ground cinnamon

1. Blend dates with water until moist. Add cinnamon and walnuts.
2. Shape into balls.
3. Roll in honey and ground almonds.

## GREEKS:

The Greeks ate dinner with their hands along with knives and spoons. They had no forks. Dairy products like cheese and yogurt were served at most meals along with bread, fruit, and olives.

### Greek Breakfast
A typical breakfast in ancient Greece consisted of:

- bread dipped in wine or grape juice
- dried figs, dates, or raisins
- olives
- cucumbers
- cheese (feta )

## ROMANS:

Wealthy Romans ate in a dining room called a triclinium, which means "three couch room." Around a central table, three couches were placed where the family and their guests lounged while eating from the table.

Guests were warned not to argue, use bad language, or flirt while eating. However, belching and spitting were allowed.

### Roman Dinner for Two
This is a modest dinner (cena in Latin) an ancient Roman would serve a guest:

*Appetizers*
- wine/grape juice sweetened with honey
- leeks, lettuce, celery, and radishes
- tuna with hardboiled egg

*Main Course*
- broccoli
- sausage
- bacon with beans
- wine or grape juice

*Dessert*
- Raisins, pears, chestnuts

137

# Dress Like an Ancient Greek, Roman, or Egyptian

Use the information below to dress like an ancient Greek, Roman, or Egyptian.

## Egypt

Braided Wig

Men wore the head scarf.

In ancient Egypt, both men and women wore thick braided wigs for special occasions. Men and women also drew dark lines around their eyes with a substance called kohl. Kohl helped reduce the glare of the sun and was thought to be healthy for the eyes. (Today, many athletes wear dark lines under their eyes for the same reason.)

## Greece

Both men and women in ancient Greece wore the same loose-fitting clothes made of wool. The wool cloth was spun and woven much lighter than today.

The tunic worn by a Greek was called a peplos. It fastened along the shoulders with long pins and was then gathered at the waist with a cord.

The cloak both men and women wore was called a himation. It was wrapped around the body with one end thrown over the shoulder. Since it was important for the himation to hang perfectly, sometimes little clay balls were sewn into the hem for weight.

Peplos

Himation

## Rome

The ancient Romans wore clothes much like those of the Greeks. The main difference was that the shoulders were completely covered by short tunics (worn by the men) or by long stola (worn by the women).

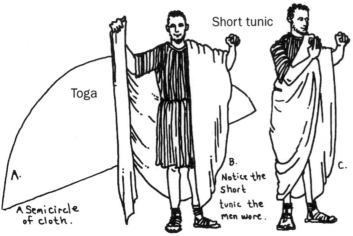

Short tunic

Toga

A.

A Semicircle of cloth.

B. Notice the short tunic the men wore.

C.

If a man were a Roman citizen, he could wear a toga. It was made of a semicircle of cloth that was three times wider than the height of the man. One end was draped over the left shoulder. The other end was wrapped under the right arm and was thrown over the left shoulder. It was then secured with a pin.

Stola

138

# Time Capsules

Follow the directions to construct your time capsule.

**Materials:**
- Student Page 140
- a two-liter plastic bottle (those used for soft drinks are best)
- artifacts (favorite objects, magazines, newspapers, audio tape, etc.)
- scissors
- tape
- permanent marking pen

*The idea of a time capsule is to capture a complete moment in the history of your life.*

**To Construct the Time Capsule:**
1. Partially cut off the top portion of a two-liter plastic bottle.
2. Fill it with the items listed on Student Page 140 as well as other artifacts. Fill out the page and gather the items that best reflect you and your life now. Add as many pictures and personal items as you wish—just make sure you can explain their significance in writing or on audio tape. Today's treasures are tomorrow's junk if you don't know the story of their significance.
3. Replace and seal the top of the bottle with tape. Write your name and the date on the outside of the time capsule.

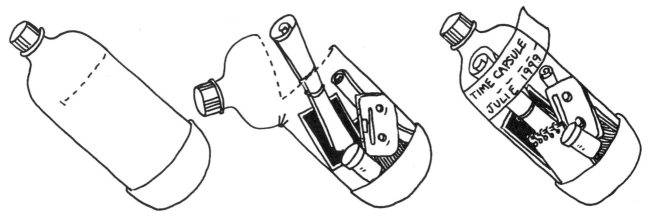

*NOTE: It is best not to bury the time capsule since moisture can damage the contents. Instead, place it in the back of a closet or a box of family treasures for future discovery.*

**Extension:**
Interview your parents, grandparents, or other people from their generation. Ask them what artifacts would reflect their life and times when they were your age. With their help or consent, construct a time capsule for them using artifacts important to them.

Name _____

*Archaeology*

## Time Capsule Questionnaire

Be specific about your answers to these questions for your time capsule.

*photo of you*

My name is _____ . Today's date is _____ .

I am in _____ grade at _____ School.

I would describe myself as _____

_____

_____

_____

_____

My favorite things to do are _____

| My friends are . . . | My favorite movies and TV shows are . . . | My favorite games, sports, and activities are . . . |
| --- | --- | --- |
| | | |

*family photo*

Here's a description of my family . . .

_____

_____

_____

_____

_____

_____

**Artifacts:** Include as many objects as you can that tell about yourself, your family, and the times in which you are living. Cut out magazine pictures, and newspaper articles. Tape record things that illustrate them, too. Include:

- photos of family, friends, and pets
- examples of personal collections (shells, baseball cards, etc.)
- significant personal items ( rabbit's foot, stuffed animal, favorite rock, jewelry, etc.)
- popular songs, groups, fads, movies, personalities/characters
- styles of clothes and hair
- important news stories and events

On the back of this paper, write about your hopes and dreams for the future, what you want to be, and how you think the world will be different in 20 years.

Name _____

# GLOSSARY

## A

**adaptation**—something that is changed or changes for a new use or situation

**aerial**—view from the air or aircraft

**aerial photography**—photographing an area from the air to detect features

**air lift**—a vacuum hose used to suck up mud from the sea bottom

**amphora**—round-bottomed pottery jar for storing liquids

**antiquities**—objects dating to ancient times

**antiquity**—ancient times

**apothecary**—a druggist or pharmacist

**architecture**—style or method of constructing buildings

**arid**—dry, parched

**artifact**—an object created or produced by humans and then left behind

## B

**balk**—wall of a square being excavated

**ballistics**—the study of projectiles; a projectile launched by hand or machine

**B.C.E.**—stands for "Before the Common Era" and replaces "B.C."

**benefactor**—person who gives financial help for a project

## C

**Carbon-14 or radiocarbon dating**—technique used to detect how much radioactive carbon (or C-14) is in an organic artifact in order to tell how long ago it died

**carbonization**—the process of burning without oxygen, which leaves the artifact charred but intact

**cartouche**—oval enclosure of royal name written in hieroglyphics

**catalogue**—to clean, number, organize, and store artifacts for study

**C.E.**—stands for "Common Era" and replaces "A.D."

**ceramic technologist**—one who studies all aspects of how and where ancient pottery was made

**chronology**—arranging events in the order in which they occurred

**codices**—volume or collection of manuscripts

**conservators**—people who conserve and preserve artifacts by processing or repairing them

**conserve**—to stabilize and preserve ancient objects so that no further decay occurs

**context**—the place or situation from which things come and how they relate to one another

**coprolites**—preserved feces

**cuneiform**—first known form of writing recorded on wet clay tablets with a wedge-shaped reed pen

## D

**decay**—to decompose or diminish

**decompose**—to break down or rot

**dendrochronologist**—one who studies tree rings

**dendrochronology**—study of tree rings to date wooden remains

**desiccate**—to dry out completely; dehydrate

**destruction layer**—layer of ruin caused by enemy attack, fire, or natural disaster such as an earthquake or volcanic activity

**diagnostics**—pieces of pottery used for analysis, including rims, collar, handle, base, and potter's marks

**domesticated animals**—tame animals that live with humans

## E

**earthwork**—an artificial mound or structure made of earth

**excavate**—to remove or expose artifacts by digging in a systematic manner

**experimental archaeology**—hands-on approach to archaeology where ancient tools and techniques are replicated

## F

**features**—permanent fixtures of a site such as postholes or cooking pits

**field**—a section or area of a site to be excavated

**find**—any archaeological discovery (used as a noun, a find)

**firing**—baking pottery in a kiln

**flotation**—means by which ancient pollen grains are found

**forensic archaeologist**—one who studies human body remains to determine such things as diet, health, age, and disease

**freeze-dry**—a way of preserving an object in which the object is frozen, then placed in a vacuum where ice is removed in the form of gas

**fresco**—painting made on a freshly plastered wall

**frieze**—sculpture carved into a wall or building

**funerary objects**—items buried with the dead

141

## G

**generation**—a span of approximately 20 years

**glyphs**—stylized picture writing (for example, the Egyptian hieroglyphs)

**ground penetrating radar (GPR)**—radar signals sent into an area to detect underground features

## H

**Heinrich Schliemann**—early archaeologist who found Troy using information from *The Iliad*

**Herculaneum**—Roman city on the other side of Mt. Vesuvius from Pompeii; also destroyed by Vesuvius' eruption

**Herodotus**—Greek historian who wrote about the ancient civilizations of the Mediterranean region

**hewn**—shaped with cutting tools

**hieroglyphics**—picture-symbol writing developed in ancient Egypt

**history**—the advent of writing demarcates history

**Homer** and **The Iliad**—Greek poet and his poem about the Trojan War

## I

**in situ**—Latin phrase meaning "in place;" excavated artifacts are recorded *in situ* before removing them from the field

**infrared photography**—type of photography that detects temperature changes caused by buried features

**inorganic**—material that never has been alive

## J

**joins**—places where potsherds fit together

**Julius Caesar**—Roman general and first emperor of Rome

## K

**kiln**—oven where pottery is heated to very high temperatures

## L

**layperson**—someone who does not have specialized training in a particular subject

**lithics** (lithic = stone)—things made of stone, such as stone tools

**locus**—locality of place; a specific location in which artifacts are found

**locus sheet**—card attached to artifacts detailing when and where they were found

## M

**marine archaeology**—excavations done on the ocean floor

**Mary Rose**—English warship (King Henry VIII's flagship), sunk over 450 years ago

**megalith**—huge stone used in building prehistoric monuments

**methodology**—methods used to excavate and interpret finds

**microorganisms**—small organisms, such as bacteria that can only be seen through a microscope

**midden**—ancient garbage pit.

**minaret**—slender tower on a mosque from which a man—the muezzin—calls Moslems to prayer

**mosaic**—picture made from small pieces of rock or glass

**mosque**—Moslem place of worship

**Mt. Vesuvius**—volcano situated between Pompeii and Herculaneum; erupted in 79 A.D. and completely destroyed both cities

**muezzin**—crier calling Moslems to prayer from a mosque's minaret

**mummified**—corpse preserved by embalming or drying

## N

**Neanderthal**—an extinct Stone Age species of human

**Neolithic** (neo = new, lithic = stone)—new Stone Age; when stone tools were finely made, polished, and specialized

**numismatist**—one who studies coins

## O

**oracle bones**—inscribed bones that are heated in order to decipher the cracks and foretell the future

**organic**—material that has once lived or is living

**ostraca**—broken piece of pottery on which there is writing

## P

**paleobotanist**—one who studies ancient plant remains and fossils

**paleographer**—one who studies ancient inscriptions and documents

**papyrus**—first form of paper, made from the papyrus plant in ancient Egypt

**parchment**—paper-like surface made from processed animal skins

**petroglyphs**—pictures etched or painted onto rocks and cliffs

**pharaoh**—ruler of ancient Egypt

**pithoi**—extremely large, heavy clay jars used to store grain and other food stuffs

**Plato**—Greek philosopher who wrote many books, including those about his teacher Socrates and the island of Atlantis

**platonic**—purely intellectual or spiritual relationship; also refers to the philosophy of Plato

**Pliny**—Roman historian who wrote accurately about the volcanic eruption that buried Pompeii

**plunder**—taking goods and money forcibly or systematically to retrieve artifacts that can be sold for profit

**polyethylene glycol (PEG)**—a liquid wax that slowly replaces water and hardens; often used to conserve wooden and leather artifacts

**Pompeii**—Roman city destroyed in 79 A.D. by the volcanic eruption of Mt. Vesuvius

**pothunters**—derogatory term used to describe grave robbers and others who disturb ancient sites

**potsherd or sherd**—broken piece of pottery

**pottery terminology**—

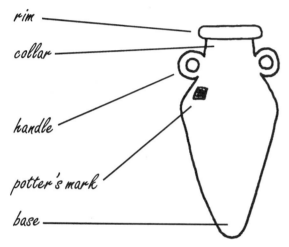

rim
collar
handle
potter's mark
base

**prehistory**—prehistory refers to time before written history

**preserve**—to keep an item intact so that it will not decay

**Pueblo Indians**—a group of Native Americans who built multi-tiered adobe or stone housing complexes in the Southwestern United States

**Q**

**quipu** (KEY-poo)—knotted strings used for primitive record keeping

**R**

**radioactive**—having atoms that decay and send out radiation

**Ramses II**—Egyptian pharaoh who lived around 1300 B.C.

**reconstruct**—to put pieces back together to form the whole artifact

**replicate**—to repeat, duplicate, or construct a copy of

**restore**—to attempt to make an artifact appear as it did originally

**S**

**scribe**—person who wrote documents, a high-ranking post in antiquity

**seal**—small inscribed stone used to imprint official documents

**Seven Wonders of the Ancient World**—architectural marvels found in the Mediterranean region and noted by the historian Herodotus

**sieve**—wire mesh used to sift excavated dirt to recover small artifacts such as beads

**site**—a place or area to be excavated

**Skara Brae**—small, ancient farming village in Scotland

**Socrates**—Greek philosopher who taught by posing questions

**sonar**—a system using sound waves bounced off underwater objects to determine their location

**square**—sites are divided and excavated in squares (usually 5- to 8-foot squares)

**stele**—stone marker or pillar inscribed with writing or pictures

**stratified site**—place people have lived for hundreds or thousands of years and built settlements, one on top of the other

**stylus**—sharp metal writing tool used by Romans to write on wax tablets

**survey**—general review of an area for archaeological features

**T**

**tel**—artificial mountain made by layers of inhabitation over centuries

**test trench**—narrow strip excavated to see if artifacts are present

**textiles**—woven or knitted fabric

**thermoluminescence (TL)**—technique used to date pottery by measuring the amount of light produced when a sample is heated to very high temperatures

**Titanic**—luxury liner that sank on its maiden voyage in 1912

**topology**—knowing typical artifacts from specific time periods.

**trowel**—small hand shovel; most commonly used archaeological tool

**U**

**utopia**—place where everything is perfect

**V**

**Vasa**—Swedish warship sunk over 350 years ago in the harbor of Stockholm

143

# Bibliography

Arnold, Guy. *Datelines of World History*. New York: Warwick, 1983.

Avi-Yonah, Michael. *Piece by Piece: Mosaics of the Ancient World*. Minnesota: Runestone, 1993.

Baquedano, Elizabeth. *Aztec, Inca & Maya*. New York: Knopf, 1993.

Beck, Barbara. *The First Book of Ancient Maya*. New York: Franklin Watts, 1965.

Bisel, Sara. *The Secrets of Vesuvius*. Toronto: Madison Press, 1990.

Branigan, Keith. *Prehistory*. New York: Warwick Press, 1984.

Briquebec, John. *The Ancient World*. New York: Warwick Press, 1990.

Cahn, Wm. & Rhoda. *The Story of Writing*. New York: Harvey House, 1963.

Caselli, Giovanni. *The First Civilizations*. New York, Bedrick Books, 1985.

Clements, Gillian. *History of the World*. New York: Farrar, Straus & Giroux, 1991.

Coblence, Jean-Michel. *Asian Civilizations*. New Jersey: Silver Burdett, 1988.

Cork, Barbara and Struan Reid. *The Young Scientist Book of Archaeology*. London: Usborne, 1984.

Corbishley, Mike. *The Ancient World*. New York: Peter Bedrick Books, 1992.

Corbishley, Mike. *Everyday Life in Roman Times*. New York: Franklin Watts, 1994.

Dawson, Imogen. *Food & Feasts in Ancient Greece*. New Jersey: New Discovery, 1995.

Delf, Brian and Richard Platt. *In the Beginning . . . : The Nearly Complete History of Almost Everything*. New York: Dorling Kindersley, 1995.

Fagg, Christopher and Frances Halton. *Atlas of the Ancient World*. New York: Warwick, 1980.

Giblin, James Cross. *The Riddle of the Rosetta Stone*. New York: Crowell, 1990.

Gibson, Michael. *Digging into the Past*. London: Hodder & Stoughton, 1975.

Gibson, Michael. *A New Look at Mysteries of Archaeology*. New York: Arco Publishing, 1980.

Glubok, Shirley. *Art and Archaeology*. New York: Harper & Row, 1966.

Gonen, Rivka. *Fired Up!: Making Pottery in Ancient Times*. Minnesota: Runestone, 1993.

Goor, Ron & Nancy. *Pompeii: Exploring a Roman Ghost Town*. New York: Crowell, 1986.

Hackwell, W. John. *Digging to the Past*. New York: Scribner's Sons, 1986.

Kan, Lai Po. *The Ancient Chinese*. New Jersey: Silver Burdett, 1981.

Lafferty, Peter and David Jefferis. *Pedal Power: The History of Bicycles*. New York: Franklin Watts, 1990.

Lessem, Dom. *The Iceman*. New York: Crown, 1994.

Lewis, Amanda. *Writing: A Fact and Fun Book*. MA: Addison-Wesley, 1992.

McEvedy, Colleen & Sarah. *The Classical World*. New York: Macmillan, 1973.

McIntosh, Dr. Jane. *Archaeology*. New York: Eyewitness Books, Knopf, 1994.

Mason, Antony. *The Children's Atlas of Civilizations*. Conn: Millbrook Press, 1994.

Pearson, Anne. *Ancient Greece*. New York: Knopf, 1992.

Pearson, Anne. *How Do We Know about the Greeks?* New York: Peter Bedrick, 1992.

Porell, Bruce. *Digging the Past*. New York: Addison-Wesley, 1979.

Putnam, James. *The Mummy*. New York: Knopf, 1993.

Rachlin, Harvey. *Lucy's Bones, Sacred Stones, & Einstein's Brain*. New York: Holt, 1996.

Rollin, Sue. *The Illustrated Atlas of Archaeology*. New York: Warwick, 1982.

Scott, Joseph & Lenore. *Egyptian Hieroglyphics for Everyone*. New York: Funk & Wagnalls, 1968.

Steele, Philip. *Food & Feasts in Ancient Rome*. New York: New Discovery, 1994.

Tucker, Louise. *The Visual Dictionary of Ancient Civilizations*. New York: Dorling Kindersley, 1994.

Unstead, R. J. *See inside an Egyptian Town*. New York: Warwick Press, 1986.

Ventura, Piero & Gian Ceserani. *In Search of Troy*. New Jersey: Silver Burdett, 1985.

Weber, Theresa Lund. *Pompeii, Herculaneum and Vesuvius*. Firenze: Bonechi, 1984.